BEAD & WIRE
art jewelry

J. Marsha
Michler

©2006 J. Marsha Michler

Published by

An Imprint of F+W Publications

700 East State Street • Iola, WI 54990-0001
715-445-2214 • 888-457-2873

Our toll-free number to place an order or obtain
a free catalog is (800) 258-0929.

The following registered trademark terms and companies appear in this publication:
Delica™, E-6000®, Fimo®, Nymo™.

Library of Congress Catalog Number: 2005935069

ISBN 13-digit: 978-0-87349-976-7
ISBN 10-digit: 0-87349-976-X

Edited by Sarah Brown
Designed by Emily Adler

Printed in the United States of America
14 13 12 11 10   8 7 6 5 4

Table of Contents

INTERMEDIATE PROJECTS

ADVANCED PROJECTS

Introduction

Your jewelry-making experience requires that you go shopping and collect some *stash*: gorgeous beads, wires and threads. Buy what strikes your fancy! If you are an absolute beginner, start by making a Classic Beaded Necklace on page 34. Make one or more, and when you feel comfortable with the wire bending process, move on to more involved pieces. Throw the very idea of achieving perfection out the window at first, and focus instead on learning how to bend, twist and wrap the individual pieces. Your work will improve the more you practice.

Many beautiful findings can be purchased, but if you are seeking handmade quality or need a part in a hurry, check the Wireworking Techniques and Findings on page 14. Ninety-nine percent of the parts you need to assemble complete pieces of jewelry can be hand made. Split rings, clasps and cord ends are just a few of the many things you can make yourself.

Use the designs in this book as inspiration. It may not be possible to find exactly the same beads that I used, so adapt the designs to suit your style and bead collection. Decide on your own unique approach to jewelry making. Seek your muse, free your soul, let your creativity dance and have fun in the making!

SAFETY FIRST

Safety is a primary consideration because of small pieces and sharp edges. Take the following precautions:

- Always wear safety glasses when working with wire.
- When cutting wire, place your hand over the cutters to prevent cut pieces from flying.
- Keep food and drink out of your workspace.
- Clean up thoroughly after each work session, keeping small beads and wire bits vacuumed up.
- Store small parts, tools and sharp pieces out of reach of young children.
- Use ventilation when using adhesives; follow the manufacturer's instructions for these substances.

As you make the projects in this book, you will notice underlined words; these are topics that have more detailed instructions in either the Wireworking Techniques and Findings section or the Beading Techniques section. Please refer to the more detailed instructions as needed.

TOOLS

Purchase the pliers, cutter, chasing hammer, jig, needle file, polishing cloth, jeweler's vise and small anvil at a jewelry supply store. You can find a cutting mat at a craft store and wire at a wire supplier or bead store.

CHAIN NOSE PLIERS
Use to bend angular shapes.

FLAT NOSE PLIERS
Use for wire wrapping to smooth wraps, and to make angular bends and flatten wire.

ROUND NOSE PLIERS
Use to make curved shapes like jump rings and split rings.

SIDE CUTTERS
Use to cut wire. Hold the pliers perpendicular to the wire and squeezing firmly. A clean cut makes a sharp "snap" sound.

CRIMPING PLIERS
Crimps "crimp" beads, usually at the beginning and end of a piece to hold beads on the wire.

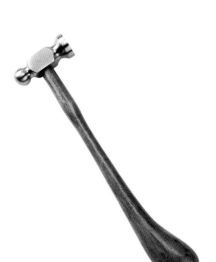

CHASING HAMMER
Use to flatten and strengthen wire.

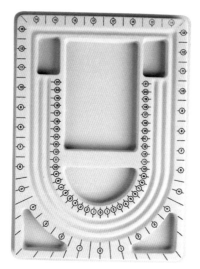

BEAD SORTING TRAY
Use to sort beads and measure the length of bracelets, necklaces, etc.

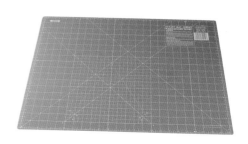

CUTTING MAT
Protects your work surface.

HAMMERING BLOCK
Surface on which to hammer wire.

JEWELER'S VISE
Holds small pieces and holds wire for twisting.

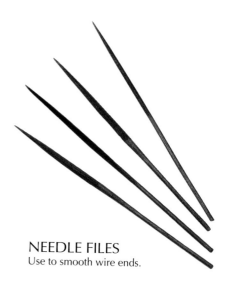

NEEDLE FILES
Use to smooth wire ends.

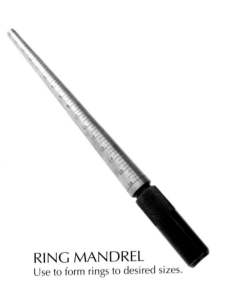

RING MANDREL
Use to form rings to desired sizes.

JIG
Use to form wire into various shapes.

BEADING TWEEZERS
Features very sharp ends for accurately making and placing knots.

WIRE TWISTING TOOL
Twists wire quickly and evenly. Use with a vise.

CROCHET HOOK, SIZE D
Use to crochet wire.

SMALL ANVIL
Surface on which to hammer wire (like hammering block).

BEADS

When you first begin to collect beads, you will be amazed at the incredible variety available. Glass beads are widely available in types ranging from factory-made to hand-made. Beads are also fashioned out of many different precious and semi-precious gemstones including agate, amethyst, aventurine, howlite, jasper, malachite, tourmaline, turquoise and a long list of others. You can also find beads made of wood, bone, horn, Fimo clay, ceramics, porcelain, seashells, metals, enameled metals (cloisonné) and other materials.

And they aren't all round. Beads come in ovals, tubes, faceted shapes, discs, rectangles, squares, triangles, carved shapes, and the natural shapes of shells and bones.

Beads are most often sized in millimeters such as 2mm, 4mm, 6mm, etc. (see the chart in the Appendix on page 127).

The hole sizes of beads are important in how they can be used. Some beads fit onto 18-gauge wire (called for in several projects), while others have much larger holes and will fit onto leather. Beads with fine holes can often be strung onto 20-gauge wire.

The smallest beads are seed beads, available in sizes such as 6/0, 8/0, 11/0, 15/0 and others, getting smaller as the numbers get larger. "/0" is pronounced, "ought." Delica seed beads are more even in size than others, creating a smooth beaded surface, and are excellent for loom beading and flat peyote stitch.

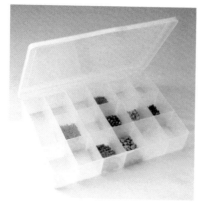

PLASTIC PORTABLE CASE
Stores beads and parts in small compartments. Find this case in a crafts store.

Bone beads. From left to right: dyed white carved with black, antique fluted, feather pendants.

Large decorative glass beads.

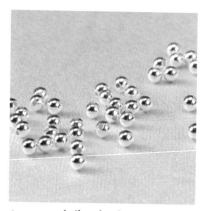

3mm round silver beads.

Semi-precious beads. From top to bottom: turquoise rondelle, amber chip, jade cube.

Shell beads. From top to bottom: blister pearl, pink rose, tiger cowry.

7mm bugle beads.

Cabochons, set and unset.

Porcelain beads.

Wood beads. From top to bottom: dark tube, black tube, natural rondelle.

Seed beads. From top to bottom: Size 6 transparent, size 15 opaque, size 11 ceylon.

Fancy silver beads. From left to right: flat square, fancy, scalloped double cone.

Pewter beads. From left to right: round with swirl, studded open round, concave tube.

6mm glass beads. From top to bottom: aurora borealis (AB) finish, regular, two-tone.

Donuts. From top to bottom: 50mm mother of pearl, 35mm Chinese writing, 25mm millefiori.

WIRE

Wire comes in various gauges, hardnesses and shapes. The most common gauges are (from lightest to heaviest) 22, 20, 18, 16 and 14. It is available in hardnesses of full hard, half-hard and dead soft. To get started with the projects in this book, use 18- and 20-gauge, dead soft, round wire. Begin with practice wire, such as brass or nickel silver, then use gold or silver for the final pieces.

Sterling silver: Both gold and silver are too soft as pure metals, so other metals are added to strengthen them. Sterling silver often consists of copper added to pure silver. This metal tarnishes.

Gold: "Karat" (k) tells how much of the metal is gold; 24k is pure gold, 14k consists of 14 parts pure gold and the remainder is an alloy, and is more durable than pure gold. Gold-filled is gold fused onto a core metal after which it is drawn out into wire.

Nickel silver: This is an alloy that often includes nickel. It appears similar to sterling silver, but is greyer in color. Unlike sterling, it does not tarnish and is often used for inexpensive findings.

Brass: This is an alloy consisting of copper and zinc. The more copper in the alloy, the more it resembles gold.

Copper: This metal has a long history of use. Wash hands after working with it, and store jewelry pieces in a dry place, since moistness creates "verdigris," which is poisonous.

Coated wire: This is a base wire with a colored coating, and is available in a range of colors and gauges.

Coated wire.

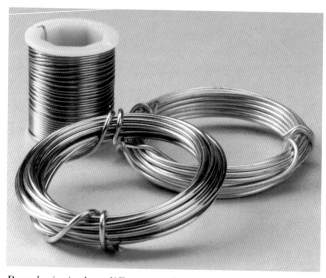

Round wire in three different metal types.

WOTWS:
Working off the wire supply. This means to work directly off of a spool or coil of wire without cutting a piece off first.

BEADING WIRES, THREADS AND NEEDLES

BEADING WIRE

Flexible beading wire.

Flexible beading wire is strong and durable, consisting of fine wires with a nylon coating. Use the finer weights for smaller beads and the heavier weights for larger beads. Wire is appropriate for semi-precious, metal and glass beads, or if your bead holes have rough surfaces. The better quality wires are more flexible and can be knotted. Using crimp beads most often finishes the ends. A needle is not needed when using beading wire.

BEADING NEEDLES

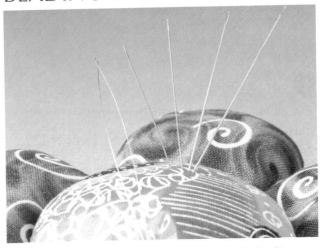

Beading needles. From left to right: open eye needle, beading needles sizes 10, 11, 12, 13.

Needle sizes, when numbered, run smaller as the number gets larger. With beading needles, the size of the bead hole and the number of times you are sewing through it indicate the size of needle to use. Keep a variety of needle sizes and types handy in case you need to change to a larger or smaller size.

BEADING THREAD

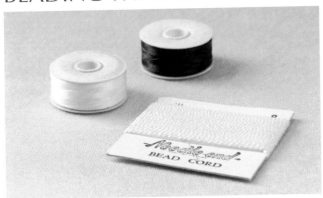

Beading thread. From left to right: white nylon beading thread, black nylon beading thread, white silk cord.

Nylon beading thread is used with seed beads for sewn and woven bead techniques. Use the finest weight when sewing many times through a bead, and heavier weights for beads with larger holes. Use a beading needle or fine sewing needle with nylon thread.

Bead cord is available in various sizes and materials. Use silk cord for stringing pearls and use nylon cord for harder stones. Match the size of the cord to the bead hole. Cord can be used single or doubled. Use a flexible beading needle - a needle made with fine, twisted wire - with cord; the eye of the needle collapses when pulling through a small bead hole.

Wireworking Techniques and Findings

FINISHING THE ENDS OF WIRE

Finishing wire ends is an essential step not only for your finished jewelry pieces, but for also preventing injury. Finish both ends of a cut piece of wire with a needle file or silicon carbide paper. When using a file, grasp the wire firmly, run the file upwards, and use a rounding stroke at the top (files should not be used backwards). Work around the wire this way, and then feel the end to be sure it is smooth.

BEAD LINKS AND DROPS

A simple loop can easily be opened up if you want to move things around. A wrapped loop uses one or more wraps around the base of a loop to create a secure connection. Only one wrap is needed, but you can add more as decorative elements; adjust the length of the wire accordingly. Use 18- or 20-gauge wire and a bead that fits the wire for the following links and drops.

Simple Loop: Bead Link

1 Cut 18-gauge wire the length of the bead plus 1", or 20-gauge wire the length of the bead plus ¾".

2 Center a bead on the wire and use a chain nose pliers to bend the wire above the bead at a 45-degree angle.

3 Grasp the wire with a round nose pliers and bend, making almost a complete circle.

4 Tighten the loop with the round nose pliers so there is no gap (this step is often done after placing the link onto another piece).

5 Repeat on the other end, or finish the end to make a drop on page 16.

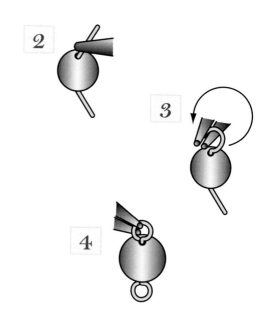

Wrapped Loop: Bead Link

1   Cut wire the length of the bead plus 2".

2   Center the bead on the wire and grasp the wire with a chain nose pliers just above the bead; bend sharply above the pliers at a 90-degree angle.

3   Remove the bead and grasp the wire just above the bend with round nose pliers; the loop will form around the nose of the pliers, so choose the place on the pliers according to the desired size of the finished loop.

4   Bend the wire over the top of the pliers. Remove the pliers.

5   Place the pliers at the top of the loop, and continue bending the loop around, shaping it around the pliers. Check that the loop is centered.

6   Clamp the round nose pliers onto the circle just made, holding it with one hand, and grasp the end of the wire with a chain nose pliers; pull the end around to create the wraps.

7   To settle the end of the wire in place, clamp a chain nose or flat-nose pliers onto the wraps lightly, and pull it around in the direction of the wraps.

8   Place the bead on the wire.

9   Finish the other end with the same wrapped loop, simple loop or drop.

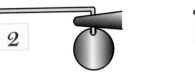

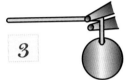

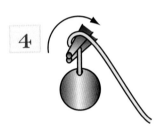

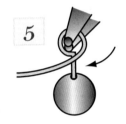

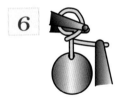

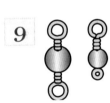

ATTACHING A WRAPPED LOOP TO ANOTHER PIECE

Before beginning the wrapped part of the loop as in Step 6 above, place the formed loop onto the piece you wish to connect it to. Grasp the loop with a round nose pliers and proceed to make the wraps as in Steps 6 and 7.

MAKE A DROP

- Hammer the remaining end flat.

- Bend a loop, coil or any shape below, with or without a bead.

POLISHING CLOTH

Before cutting a length of wire off the wire supply, run a polishing cloth over the wire to straighten it. Polish your finished wire pieces first using the rouge side of the cloth (rouge is a polishing agent used by jewelers), then using the plain flannel side.

CONNECTOR AND END CAP

To finish a multi-strand piece, a connector and end cap are used at each end.

Connector

Connectors are handy wherever you need a secure connection at one end and a removable one at the other. Use 20- or 18-gauge wire.

1 Cut 1½" of wire, and make a wrapped loop using 1" of one end.

2 Make a simple loop using the remaining ½."

End Cap

Add an end cap over the loose ends of a multi-strand piece to cover the spot where the multiple strands meet. This gives the ends a neater finish. Use 20-, 18- or 16-gauge wire for the end cap.

1 Using a round nose pliers and WOTWS, bend a small loop and continue to bend the wire around, making the loops larger as you continue to loop the wire around, and keeping the loops snug against each other.

2 Check that the piece fits over one loop of the connector and the multiple strands, and is long enough to cover it.

CHAINS

Simple Chain

This is a simple way to make a chain. Use 18-gauge wire. This chain is shown on page 38. Use it with the Simple Hook & Loop Clasp on page 19.

1 Cut 1" lengths of 18-gauge wire.

2 Use a round nose pliers to bend one end to the back.

3 Bend the other end to the side using the round nose pliers.

4 Make a second link, and while closing the link, place it onto the first one, and continue, making the chain the length desired.

Eyelet Chain

Form rounded links over a dowel or elongated links over a round nose pliers. Use 18- or 20-gauge wire. This chain is shown on page 44. See Eyelet Chain Clasp on page 20.

1 Cut 1½" lengths of wire for smaller links, and 1¾" lengths for larger links.

2 Form the eyelet part of the link over a dowel or other rounded object with your hands.

3 Bend the ends so they come together using a chain nose or flat nose pliers.

4 Hammer the rounded part of the link to flatten (optional).

5 Use a round nose pliers to form the loose ends into simple loops, fastening them on to the eyelet part of the previous link.

6 Continue these steps to make the chain the length desired.

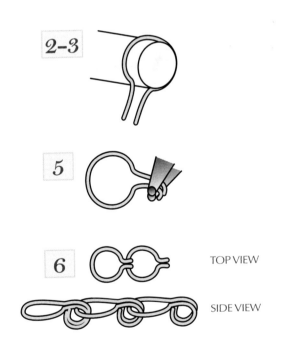

TOP VIEW

SIDE VIEW

Hammered Link Chain

Vary the length of the wire from 1" to 1½" or even longer, depending on the look you wish to achieve. Use 20- and 18-gauge wire. Shown on page 50.

1 Cut 1¼" lengths of 18-gauge wire.

2 Hammer the center of the wire (but not the ends) to flatten slightly.

3 Bend the ends into simple loops to the back using a round nose pliers.

4 Use the 20-gauge wire to make <u>split rings</u>. (See page 21).

5 Attach the links together, using a round nose pliers to open and close the loops of the hammered links; begin and end the chain with a split ring.

CLASPS

"S" Clasp

This clasp is one piece and works well for necklaces and bracelets. Use 18-gauge wire.

1 Cut a 1½" length of wire.

2 Shape the wire according to the diagram using a round nose pliers.

3 Lay the wire on an anvil and give it a few taps with a chasing hammer to harden the metal and flatten slightly.

Simple Hook and Loop Clasp

Use this clasp with the simple chain, other self-made chains and bead-strung pieces. Use 18-gauge wire.

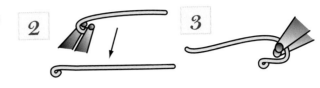

CLASP HOOK

1 Cut a 1½" length of wire.

2 Use a chain nose pliers to sharply bend the tip of the wire and flatten it as tightly as possible against the wire to make the decorative end.

3 Bend the same end into a larger "catch" loop.

4 Finish the other end by bending an upward loop to fasten onto the jewelry.

CLASP LOOP

1 Cut a 1¾" length of wire.

2 Bend a small loop on one end for fastening onto jewelry.

3 Form the "loop" of the clasp by making a wide loop with the wire.

4 Finish the other end by bending another loop, fastening it near the loop made in Step 2.

Split Ring Clasp

The doubled wire matches a split ring. Use a split ring as the clasp loop. Use 18-gauge wire. See Split Ring on page 21.

1 Cut a 3" length of 18-gauge wire.

2 Bend the wire in half.

3 Using a round nose pliers, bend the open ends into a loop for attaching, bending both wires at the same time.

4 Shape the other end into a clasp hook using a round nose pliers.

Eyelet Chain Clasp

Use this clasp with the eyelet chain. Use 18-gauge wire.

1 Cut a 2½" length of 18-gauge wire.

2 Form the eyelet part of the clasp over a dowel or other rounded object by hand. Use a chain nose or flat nose pliers to bring the ends together. Remove the wire from the dowel.

3 Using a round nose pliers, bend back the ends of the wire sharply, then form the clasp shape.

4 Fasten the clasp onto the doubled bent loops of the final link of the eyelet chain.

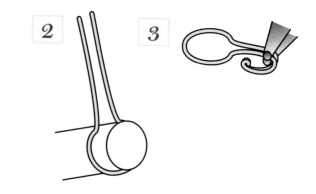

Toggle Clasp

A toggle clasp is used by turning the bar sideways to fit it through the loop end of the clasp. Use 14-gauge wire and 18- or 20-gauge wire. A Toggle Clasp is shown on page 53.

1 Cut a 1" length of 14-gauge wire.

2 Cut a 3" length of 18-gauge wire or 4" of 20-gauge wire.

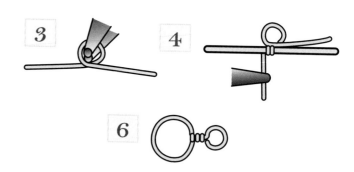

3 Using a round nose pliers, bend a small loop at the center of the 18- or 20-gauge wire.

4 Tightly wrap each end around the 14-gauge wire using a chain nose pliers.

5 Cut 2½" of 18- or 20-gauge wire.

6 Use this piece to make a connector, using 2" to make a <u>large wrapped loop</u> and the remaining ½" into a simple loop.

JUMP RINGS

Jump rings can be made the same way as split rings except the finished piece is a single thickness.

To use jump rings, open and shut the cut ends by swiveling the ends away from each other then back together instead of pulling the ends outwards. This helps to retain the strength of the wire and the shape of the loop.

COILS

Flat Coil Spacer, Drop and Bead Cap

Use closed coils for spacer beads, or make them into drops or bead caps. Only coil as far as the piece will hold its shape. Use 18- or 20-gauge wire.

1 WOTWS, make a small simple loop using a round nose pliers.

2 Grab onto the loop with chain nose or flat nose pliers and pull the wire around by hand so it snugs up against the loop, continuing until the coil is complete.

3 Hammer gently to set the coil (optional).

4 Finish as desired. Here are some suggestions:

To make a drop, turn the outer end into a loop using a round nose pliers.

To make an open coil, leave some space between the coils.

To make a bead cap, grip the center with a round nose and pull gently outwards until the coil fits the bead.

Split Ring

Split rings can also be made using a round nose pliers by turning the pliers, although it is difficult to make two alike this way. Use 18- or 20-gauge wire. A Split Ring Chain is shown on page 41.

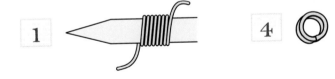

1 WOTWS, wrap the wire around a knitting needle or dowel.

2 Cut off the excess wire with the wire cutter.

3 Remove the coiled piece from the knitting needle.

4 Pull the coils apart enough to cut the coil into sections. Make cuts so each split ring has doubled wire.

5 Hold each split ring in a round nose pliers and file the cut ends smooth using a needle file.

6 After placing a split ring onto the jewelry piece, use a round nose or chain nose pliers to nudge the coils close together.

Coil Bead

Use coil beads for spacers, bead links, or string them like beads. To make a fine bead, I like to use a size 0000 knitting needle or a nail. Use 20- or 18-gauge wire.

COIL BEAD

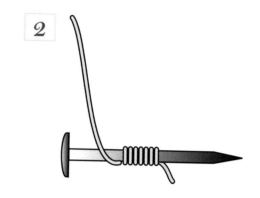

1 WOTWS, bend wire 1"-2" from the end, and hold the bend tightly against a nail or knitting needle.

2 Wrap the wire so the wraps are snugly against each other, and repeat with the beginning of the wire. (This is the same as steps 3, 4, and 5 on page 15).

3 Cut the wire when the bead is the length desired.

Cord Ends

Use cord ends to neatly finish fiber or leather strands. For fibers other than leather, place glue or nail polish on the fibers before wrapping. Use 18- or 20-gauge wire.

1 Cut 3" of wire; bend the wire at a 90-degree angle ¼" from one end using a chain nose pliers.

2 Place the round nose pliers just next to the 90-degree bend. Bend a loop (upward and around), as shown in the diagram.

3 Place the loop onto the leather or fiber and grip with a round nose pliers; the leather should be longer than needed so the pliers will grip it. Use tape to hold the leather together.

4 Wrap the ¼" section of the wire and the leather, then press the final wrap lightly into the leather (do not let the wire cut into the leather).

5 Trim off the excess leather using a sharp-pointed scissors.

FORMING WIRE

Jig Shapes

Many wire shapes can be made using a round nose pliers, but jigs work well for making repeated shapes or loopy shapes characteristic of peg wrapping. An example of this is the Triple-Loop Bracelet on page 46.

1 Bend the wire into a loop to fit on a peg of the jig.

2 Wrap the wire around the pegs to create the shape desired using the end of a wooden dowel to push the wire down as needed.

3 Remove the piece from the pegs and hammer gently if needed to set the loops.

Braiding Wire

Use a bench vise to keep a tight hold on the wires. Make braids with any multiple of three strands. Use 20-gauge wire and a 3" length of 18- or heavier gauge wire.

1 Cut the 20-gauge wire into strands, each a little more than the length needed.

2 Turn a loop into one end of each using a round nose pliers, and fasten onto the 18-gauge wire.

3 Bend the larger wire ends to the back and place securely into the vise.

4 Separate the 20-gauge strands into three equal sections, and begin braiding, keeping the wire strands parallel to each other; you may find it helpful to use a chain nose pliers to pull each strand (separately) into place.

5 If desired, hammer the braided piece very gently; this will help to "set" the wires.

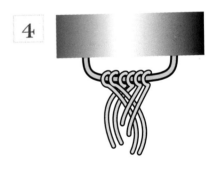

Twisting Wire

1 Cut two wires the same length and fasten into a bench vise.

2 Use a twisting tool or a pair of pliers and twist until the wires are well twisted. Or, fasten the ends into pin vises and twist.

EAR WIRES

Basic Ear Wire

Learn to make ear wires using 20-gauge practice wire (brass, copper or nickel silver). Make finished ear wires using sterling silver or gold wire in 21- or 22-gauge.

1 Cut 1½" of wire and bend a loop using a round nose pliers.

2 Shape the remainder of the ear wire according to the diagram.

3 File, or use silicon carbide paper to make the end very smooth.

4 Make a second one to match.

More Ear Wire Shapes

Each style will require its own length of wire. Design ear wires in practice wire (20-gauge) using specific lengths of wire such as 2", 3", etc. That way, you will be able to make a second earring or additional pairs the same.

WRAPPING

Wrapping with Half-Round Wire

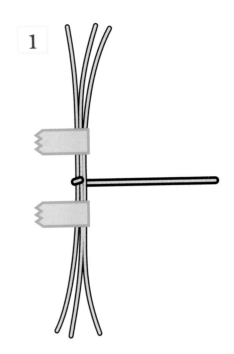

1 Secure the wires to be wrapped with masking tape, then WOTWS, bend the end of the wrapping wire sharply and place it on the wires to be wrapped.

2 Clamp a flat nose or chain nose pliers onto the end, and bring the half round wire around the wires by hand, flattening each wrap as you make them. End on the wrong side.

Wrapping with Round Wire

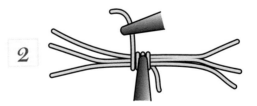

1 Cut 1¼" of 20-gauge round wire, bend the wire in half, place it around the piece to be wrapped and clamp it with a flat nose pliers.

2 Using a chain nose pliers, bend one end around until the wire is used up. Repeat with the other end. Wrap until the wire is used up or until the number of wraps needed.

Beading Techniques

CRIMPING

Crimp beads are used to secure the ends of flexible beading wire. After making the crimp, check that the wires do not slip. The instructions below use a crimping pliers, but you can also close a crimp bead by squeezing it with a flat nose pliers. You will need flexible beading wire, two crimp beads, two clasp findings and a crimping pliers.

1 String the beads onto the beading wire leaving 3"-4" of wire at each end.

2 String one crimp bead and half of the clasp finding onto one end.

3 Run the end of the wire back through the crimp bead and through several beads; pull up on the wire to position the crimp next to the finding.

4 Using the crimping pliers, flatten the crimp bead with the double-indented opening (toward the back of the pliers).

5 Using the crimping pliers, place the crimp bead in the rounded area towards the front and squeeze. This rounds the crimp bead.

6 Trim the end of the wire to hide neatly under the beads.

7 Use the crimping pliers, crimp bead and the other half of the clasp finding to finish the other end of the wire, following Steps 1-6.

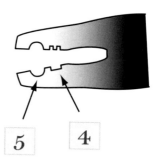

5   4

BEAD TIP

A bead tip is a small finding used to conceal knots at the ends of bead cords. Use the loop at the top to fasten on a link, jump ring or clasp.

KNOTTING BEAD CORD

Knotted Strand Using Bead Tips

Bead tips make a neat finish for the ends of strung jewelry, making it easy to fasten on a clasp or other finding. You will need nylon bead cord, a flexible beading needle, and beads to complete your project, two bead tips, clear nail polish and a beading tweezers. (See Pearl Necklace on page 80).

1 Cut bead cord five times the desired length of the necklace. Fold in half so it is doubled. (Note: for clarity, the doubled thread is not shown in the illustrations).

2 Place the needle on the doubled end.

3 Tie a surgeon's knot at the loose ends.

4 String a bead tip onto the cord, followed by the remaining beads.

5 Slide a bead up to the bead tip and form an overhand knot after the bead, leaving the knot loose.

6 With the tweezers inside the knot, grasp the bead cord next to the bead and tighten the knot around the tweezers.

7 Carefully slide the tweezers out, and then use it to push the knot toward the bead while tightening the knot.

8 Knot between each bead until the final bead.

9 Slide the final bead up to the last knot, and string on a bead tip.

10 Make a surgeon's knot after the bead tip, and use the tweezers to place it inside the bead tip.

11 Saturate the knots in the bead tips with clear nail polish, allow to dry thoroughly, and clip the thread ends.

5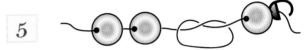

6

7

SURGEON'S KNOT

A surgeon's knot is the same as an overhand knot (like tying a shoe), except bring the thread through the large loop a second time.

Knotted Strand Using Bullion

Using bullion, or French coil, a finely coiled wire tube, is a classy way to finish the ends of jewelry strung onto bead cord. Handle bullion carefully, as it is delicate. See Knotted Strand Using Bead Tips on page 27 for knotting instructions. You will need size 1 beading cord, a flexible beading needle, beads to complete your project, clasp or bead link, clear nail polish or glue and two ¼" lengths of silver bullion. (See Coral and Turquoise Necklace on page 106).

1   Cut the beading cord three times the desired length of the necklace.

2   Tie a loose knot about 3" from one end and place the needle onto the other end.

3   Set aside the first three beads and string on all of the rest, keeping the beads about 12" away from the knot.

4   String on a piece of bullion and a clasp or a link, then go through the final bead and pull the thread through, pulling the bullion into a loop.

5   Knot next to the final bead.

6   Run the needle through the following bead, knot again, and continue to the beginning of the strand.

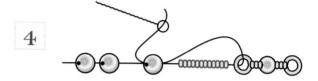

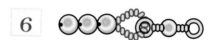

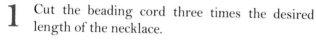

7   Remove the needle.

8   Remove the loose knot made in Step 2; place the needle on the thread.

9   String on the remaining three beads, and follow Steps 4-6, removing the needle after going through the third bead.

10   Hold the two thread ends together and tie them in an overhand knot.

11   Place glue or clear nail polish on the knot and trim the ends.

PEYOTE STITCH

This stitch gives beads the appearance of stacked bricks. It is an easy stitch to learn and do. You will need 11/0 seed beads, nylon beading thread, a beading needle or fine sewing needle and beeswax. (See the Assemblage Necklace on page 114).

1 Cut one yard of beading thread.

2 Run the beading thread over the beeswax, which will prevent the ends from fraying and allow beads to thread with ease.

3 Thread on the beading needle or fine sewing needle.

4 Rows 1 and 2: String on an even number of beads, using twice as many as you will have in each row.

5 Row 3: String on one bead and sew through the second bead of the beginning strand, string another, skip one and sew through the next one, and continue across the row.

6 To begin a new row, turn the work, string on a bead and sew through the topmost bead of the previous row, string another and sew through the next topmost bead, and continue across.

7 To fasten off, run the thread through a few beads, tie a knot, and run the thread through several more beads, then trim the thread end.

4

5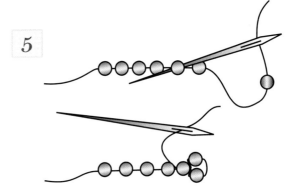

6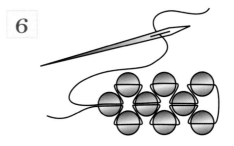

Peyote Tube Beads

Flat peyote stitch makes wonderful tube-shaped beads. Used in the flat format (rather than circular), the beading is snug and tight. (Shown in the Assemblage Necklace on page 114).

1 String on the number of beads needed to make the desired length of beaded bead.

2 Work an even number of rows, following the peyote stitch steps above.

3 Using the same thread, sew the top and bottom edges together, and fasten off.

EMBROIDERY

For an embroidery background, use lightweight leather, imitation suede or a commercially available stiffened material especially made for beading. Embroidered pieces should be backed with leather or other material to cover thread ends and any metal pieces that are inserted. Use a beading needle or fine sewing needle and nylon beading thread. Wax the thread using beeswax. Begin by knotting the thread and fastening securely to the embroidery background. (See the Embroidered Cuff on page 116).

Backstitch

1 String on several beads (typically two to six), and sew them down at the end of the line of beads.

2 Come up at the center of the line of beads and sew through the end beads. String on the same number of beads as before and repeat.

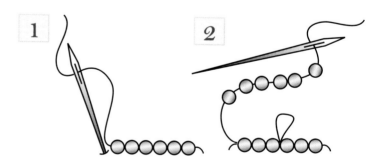

30

Bead Fringe

String on two or more beads, skip the top one, and sew back down through the remaining beads.

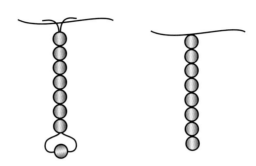

Beaded Bezel

Rows of Peyote stitching are worked so they appear to hold a cabochon in place. See Peyote Stitch on page 29. (Shown in the Embroidered Cuff on page 116).

Note: Cut the backing material slightly larger than the finished piece; complete the stitching, then carefully cut the backing to size.

1 Use an industrial-strength glue, such as E6000, to glue a cabochon to the background material. Allow to completely dry before stitching.

2 Backstitch a row of seed beads around the base of the cabochon. (See Backstitch on page 30).

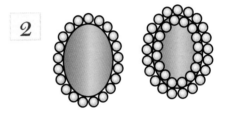

3 String on one bead and begin Peyote stitch working into the backstitched base row.

4 Continue working Peyote stitch for three to four rows, decreasing as needed so the stitching hugs the stone.

Ladder Stitch

Ladder Stitch is used in the Embroidered Cuff on page 116.

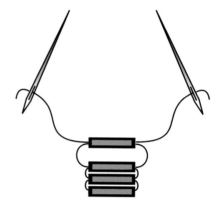

1 Cut a length of nylon beading thread, wax it and place a needle on each end.

2 String on one bead (bugle beads are shown here), then run the needles through a second bead, each needle going the opposite direction, and repeat to add on each new bead.

Loom Beading

The Tapestry Pin and Earrings on page 118 are examples of Loom Beading. Use a charted design or work freely as shown in the Tapestry Pin.

1 Thread the loom according to the manufacturer's instructions using one more thread than the number of beads in the row, and stringing the warp to have at least 7" left at each end to weave in the threads later.

2 String the first row of beads in the same order as given in the chart. Hold the strung beads under the warp threads on the loom and push them up with your finger so they are between the threads and spaced evenly.

3 Sew through the beads above the warp threads. Continue until you have reached your desired length.

4 To finish, remove the piece from the loom, thread each warp end into a needle and work the ends into the weaving.

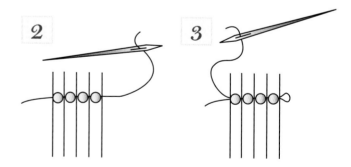

Crocheted Chain

Crochet is simply using a hook to pick up fiber or wire and pulling it through the loop on the hook. It is easy to learn, and working in wire creates an airy, light chain. After making a chain, "set" it by giving a couple of sharp tugs on the length of it; then your jewelry won't stretch out after it is made. You will need 28-gauge wire and a size D crochet hook. A crocheted chain bracelet and necklace are shown on pages 76 and 78.

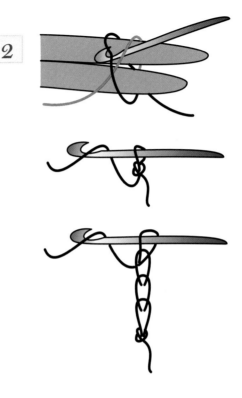

1   Make a slipknot: wrap the wire around your fingers, then wrap again behind the first wrap.

2   Slip the hook under the first wrap, pull the second one through, then pull the knot snug.

3   Holding onto the tail, catch the wire with the hook and pull the hook through, keeping the new loop about the size of the hook. Repeat until you have reached your desired length.

4   To fasten off, run the wire end through the final chain loop and pull tight.

Lark's Head Knot

A simple and attractive knot can be made in cord or a fine wire. This knot is shown in leather on page 74, and in wire on page 107.

1   Double the tying material, creating a loop.

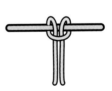

2   Place the object on top, and bring the loose ends through the loop.

Classic Beaded Necklace

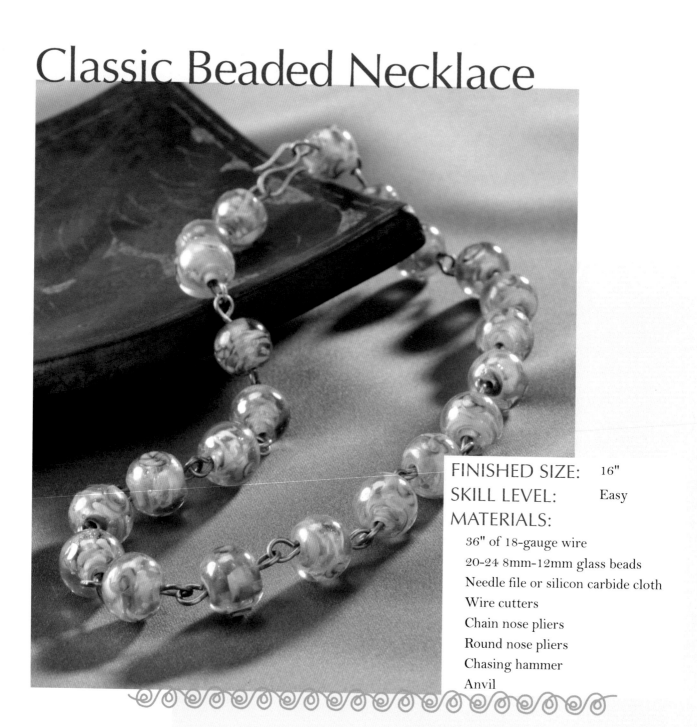

FINISHED SIZE: 16"
SKILL LEVEL: Easy
MATERIALS:

   36" of 18-gauge wire
   20-24 8mm-12mm glass beads
   Needle file or silicon carbide cloth
   Wire cutters
   Chain nose pliers
   Round nose pliers
   Chasing hammer
   Anvil

The classic bead link necklace is the ultimate beginner project.
Use this project to start your wireworking experience.

INSTRUCTIONS

1 Using a wire cutters, cut lengths of wire the length of the bead plus 1".

2 Smooth the ends of the wire using a file or silicon carbide cloth.

3 With one length of wire, make a <u>simple bead link.</u>

4 Using a second length of wire, make a second simple bead link; after bending the loops at the ends, open one end slightly, place it onto the first bead link and tighten the loop.

5 Continue making links and connecting them until the necklace is the length desired.

MAKE AND ATTACH THE CLASP

1 Cut 1½" of 18-gauge wire. Make an <u>"S" clasp</u>.

2 Place the "S" clasp on the end loops of the necklace.

Variation

Crystal Beaded Strand

FINISHED SIZE: 19"

SKILL LEVEL: Easy

MATERIALS:

15 feet of 20-gauge wire

160 size 8/0 crystal seed beads

Clasp

Needle file or silicon carbide cloth

Wire cutters

Chain nose pliers

Round nose pliers

Sparkly crystal beads and silver wire give this necklace an airy look. This is a great project to practice making beaded links; each link consists of one simple and one wrapped loop.

MAKE THE CHAIN

1 Cut 1⅜" of wire. Make a <u>bead link</u> using one seed bead; wrap one end and make a simple loop at the other.

2 Cut 1½" of wire. Make a bead link using two seed beads and finishing the ends as in Step 1.

3 Continue to make links and fasten them together as they are made with a chain nose pliers, alternating the one-bead and two-bead links. Make a length 18½" long.

ASSEMBLE THE NECKLACE

1 Make a second strand 7" long and fasten it onto the first, as shown in the diagram.

2 Make a third strand 11" long and fasten it onto the first, as shown in the diagram.

3 Make a fourth strand 15" long, and fasten it onto the first, as shown in the diagram.

4 Attach a clasp to the original 18½" strand.

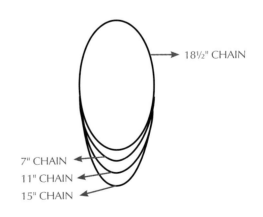

18½" CHAIN

7" CHAIN
11" CHAIN
15" CHAIN

Pearl Cluster Necklace

FINISHED SIZE: 16"

SKILL LEVEL: Easy

MATERIALS:

4¼ feet of 18-gauge wire

1 16" strand each of 6mm, 8mm and 10mm glass pearls

9 feet of 20-gauge wire

"S" clasp

Needle file or silicon carbide cloth

Wire cutters

Chain nose pliers

Round nose pliers

Chasing hammer

Anvil

Hammered coils highlight the clustered pearls in this elegant necklace. Vary this project by your choice of beads and the number you attach to each chain link.

MAKE THE CHAIN

1 Cut 16 lengths of 18-gauge wire, each 1¼"; make a <u>simple chain</u> 6" long.

2 Cut 15 lengths of 18-gauge wire, each 1"; make two <u>simple chains</u>, each 5" long.

3 Attach one 5" chain to each end of the 6" center chain.

MAKE THE SIMPLE BEAD DROPS

1 Cut the following lengths from the 20-gauge wire:

NAME	QUANTITY	LENGTH
Drop A	16	2"
Drop B	12	1¾"
Drop C	36	1½"

2 With one length of wire and one bead each, make <u>simple bead drops</u>, attaching the 10mm beads to the 2" wire to create Drop A, the 8mm beads to the 1¾" wire to create Drop B, and the 6mm beads to the 1½" wire to create Drop C. Hammer the ends and coil them tightly against the beads.

ASSEMBLE THE NECKLACE

1 Attach two of Drop A to each loop of the eight center chain links.

2 Attach two of Drop B to each of the next three loops, placing six on each side of the necklace.

3 Attach two of Drop C to each of the remaining loops, on either side of the necklace, spacing the final drops on each side farther apart on the chain. Leave approximately 3½" of chain on each end of the necklace.

4 Attach the clasp.

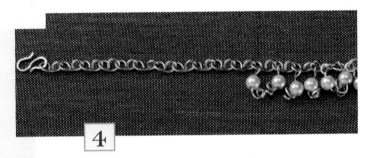

4

Hammered Links Bracelet and Earrings

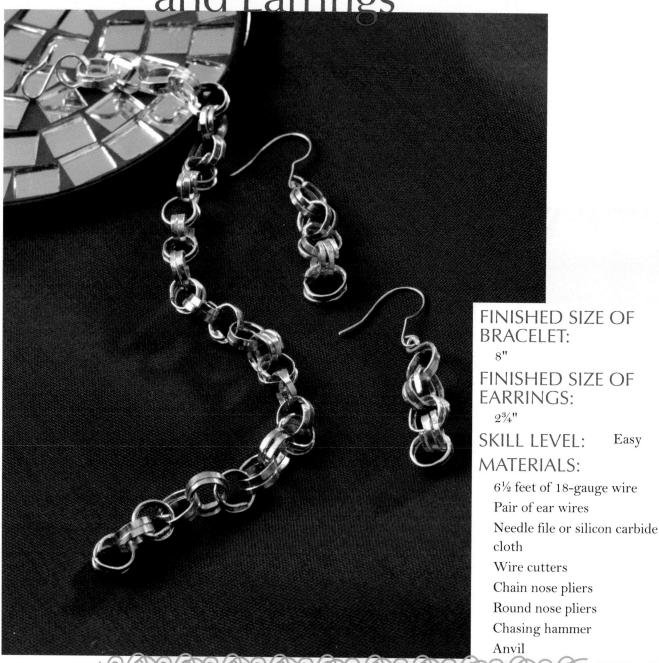

FINISHED SIZE OF BRACELET:
8"

FINISHED SIZE OF EARRINGS:
2¾"

SKILL LEVEL: Easy

MATERIALS:

6½ feet of 18-gauge wire

Pair of ear wires

Needle file or silicon carbide cloth

Wire cutters

Chain nose pliers

Round nose pliers

Chasing hammer

Anvil

Hammered wire makes a classy variation on split ring chain. A plain Split Ring Chain is shown on page 41.

Bracelet

MAKE THE CHAIN

1 Cut 32 lengths of wire, each 1¾".

2 Using the chasing hammer and anvil, hammer each length of wire until it is about 2" long.

3 Coil each length of hammered wire into a <u>split ring</u> using the widest part of the round nose pliers; attach one link to another as they are made. Continue until the bracelet is the length desired.

MAKE AND ATTACH THE CLASP

1 Cut a 3" length of wire.

2 Using the round nose pliers, bend a tiny part of one end of the wire to the side tightly and hammer it. (Similar to the Simple Clasp Hook on page 19).

3 Shape the bent end into a clasp, and the other into a split ring.

4 Attach the clasp to the chain.

Variation

Earrings

1 Cut four lengths of wire, each 1¾"; make four hammered <u>Split Rings</u> same as above, attaching them together.

2 Make one more split ring from a 2" length of wire, but before hammering it, bend the top into a <u>simple loop</u>.

3 Hammer the remaining length and form it into a split ring; fasten it to the top of the linked rings.

4 Attach an ear wire.

5 Repeat Steps 1-4 to make a second earring.

Burma Jade
Bracelet and Earrings

FINISHED SIZE OF BRACELET:
8¼"

FINISHED SIZE OF EARRINGS:
1¼"

SKILL LEVEL: Easy

MATERIALS:

12 Burma jade 6mm beads

6 feet of 18-gauge wire

6" of 21- or 22-gauge wire

Needle file or silicon carbide cloth

Wire cutters

Chain nose pliers

Round nose pliers

Chasing hammer

Anvil

The wrapped bead links add character to this bracelet featuring Burma jade beads.

Bracelet

1 From the 18-gauge wire, cut 10 lengths, each 2" longer than a bead.

2 Make 10 <u>wrapped bead links</u>.

3 WOTWS, make <u>split rings</u> out of 18-gauge wire, and attach them between beaded links.

4 Make an <u>"S" clasp</u> out of 18- gauge wire; attach it to the chain.

3

Earrings

1 Cut 3" of 21- or 22-gauge wire.

2 Make a tiny <u>wrapped loop</u> at one end.

3 Add two beads, and a small <u>coil bead</u> made from 18-gauge wire.

4 Shape the remainder of the wire into an <u>ear wire</u>.

5 Repeat the instructions to make a second earring.

Rhodonite Drops Necklace

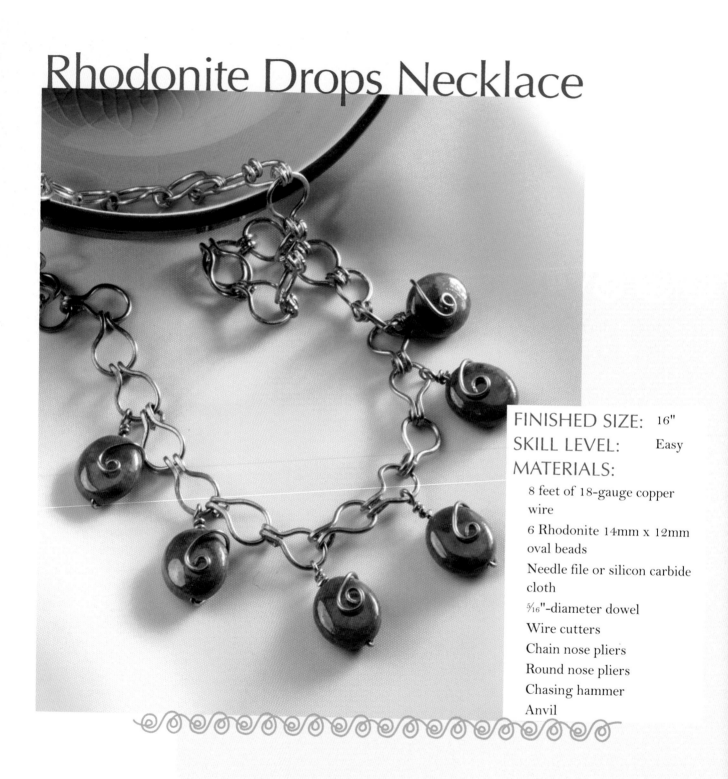

FINISHED SIZE: 16"
SKILL LEVEL: Easy
MATERIALS:

8 feet of 18-gauge copper wire

6 Rhodonite 14mm x 12mm oval beads

Needle file or silicon carbide cloth

5/16"-diameter dowel

Wire cutters

Chain nose pliers

Round nose pliers

Chasing hammer

Anvil

Rhodonite is a pinkish-red stone that goes well with copper. Add as many drops as you like.

MAKE THE CHAIN

1 Cut 38 lengths of wire, each 1¾".

2 Use the 1¾" lengths to make an <u>eyelet chain</u>, forming the rounded portion over the dowel, and hammering the links.

MAKE THE BEAD DROPS

1 Cut six lengths of wire, each 3".

2 Make six <u>wrapped bead drops</u> using one length of wire and one bead for each; bend the wire end up onto the bead and curl it decoratively on the bead; fasten each drop onto an eyelet chain link as you complete it.

MAKE AND ATTACH THE CLASP

Make and attach an <u>eyelet chain clasp</u>.

Variations

Use this same method to make a hammered chain, and then add a pendant. The eyelet chain also looks great with a wider link and is eye-catching enough to stand alone.

Triple-Loop Bracelet

FINISHED SIZE: 7½"
SKILL LEVEL: Easy
MATERIALS:

- 5 feet of 18-gauge wire
- Wire cutters
- Jig
- Needle file or silicon carbide cloth
- Chain nose pliers
- Round nose pliers
- Dowel, any size
- Chasing hammer
- Anvil

This chain-link design is easy to make on a jig. Before cutting all of the wire, cut one piece and try it on the jig to be sure the design turns out correctly.

MAKE THE CHAIN

1 Cut 16 lengths of wire, each 3¼".

2 Using the jig, bend each length of wire into the triple loop pattern, as shown.

3 Hammer each link gently.

4 Bend each link over a dowel to round it slightly, giving it a bit of dimension.

5 Using a round nose pliers, bend the two ends of each link into a <u>simple loop</u> for fastening; join the links together.

MAKE AND ATTACH THE CLASP

1 To make the clasp loop, cut 3¾" of wire.

2 Bend it on the jig, following the pattern, but making the center loop about twice as large as before; fasten it to the bracelet.

3 To make the hook, cut 4" of wire.

4 Bend on the jig, following the pattern; fasten it to the other end of the bracelet.

5 Using a round nose pliers, bring the two ends of the hook together; turn tight, small loops, and bend to form the clasp.

Graceful Chain Bracelet

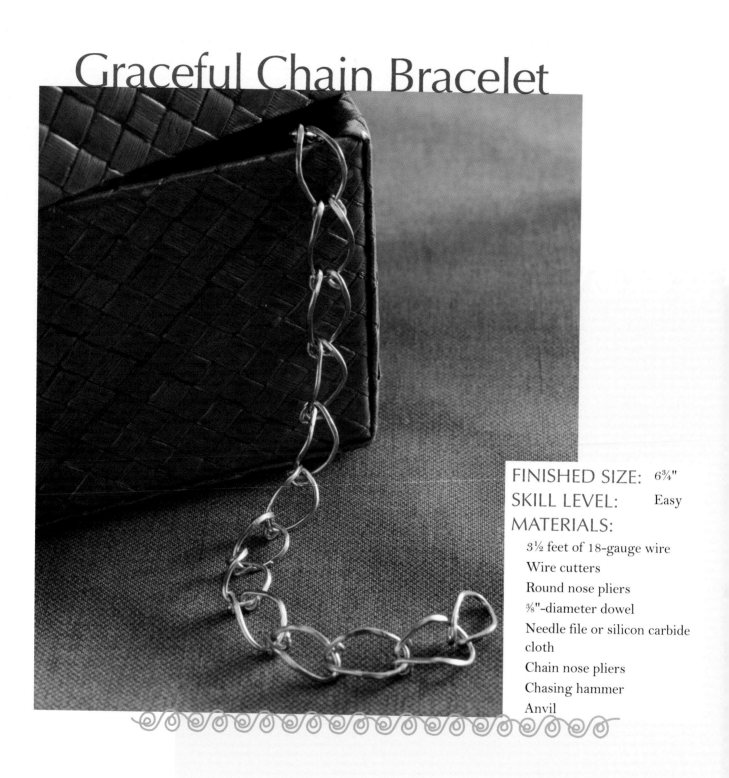

FINISHED SIZE: 6¾"

SKILL LEVEL: Easy

MATERIALS:

3½ feet of 18-gauge wire

Wire cutters

Round nose pliers

⅜"-diameter dowel

Needle file or silicon carbide cloth

Chain nose pliers

Chasing hammer

Anvil

This chain is similar to the eyelet chain, but the rounded links add dimension.

MAKE THE CHAIN

1 Cut 13 lengths of wire, each 2".

2 One at a time, grasp each length at its center with a round nose pliers and bend sharply.

3 Gently bend the two sides around a dowel until the free ends meet.

4 Grasp the piece by the bend and hammer gently.

5 Bend the link over a dowel to form a gentle curve.

6 Using a round nose pliers, bend each loose end into a small loop. Assemble the links as they are made.

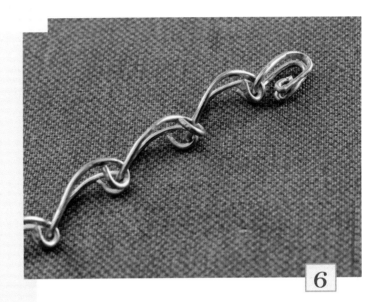

MAKE AND ATTACH THE CLASP

Make and attach an eyelet chain clasp, forming it to match the links of the chain.

Beaded Links Necklace

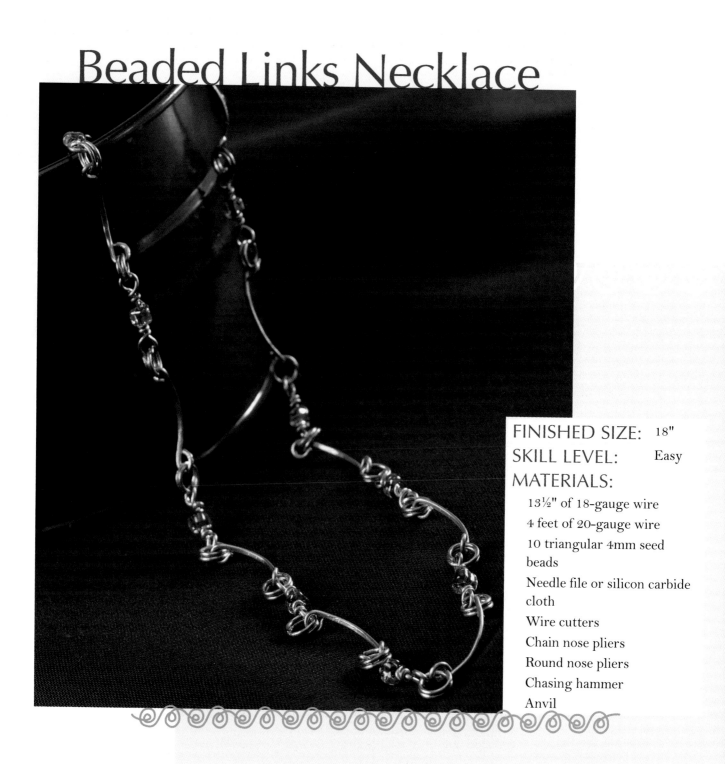

FINISHED SIZE: 18"

SKILL LEVEL: Easy

MATERIALS:

13½" of 18-gauge wire

4 feet of 20-gauge wire

10 triangular 4mm seed beads

Needle file or silicon carbide cloth

Wire cutters

Chain nose pliers

Round nose pliers

Chasing hammer

Anvil

A variation on the hammered link chain makes an elegant and delicate-looking necklace.

MAKE THE TWISTED LINKS

1 Cut nine lengths of 18-gauge wire, each 1½".

2 Hammer each length to flatten slightly.

3 Bend the ends into small loops using a round nose pliers.

4 Bend each link into a half-moon shape.

5 Using a pliers in each hand, rotate one end so one end loop faces up and the other faces down, giving each link a twist at the center.

6 Line the links up on your work space so they are all aligned the same way.

MAKE THE WRAPPED BEAD LINKS

1 Cut 10 lengths of 20-gauge wire, each 2¼".

2 Make 10 <u>wrapped bead links</u> using one triangular seed bead per link.

MAKE AND ATTACH THE SPLIT RINGS

1 WOTWS, make 20 <u>split rings</u> out of the 20-gauge wire.

2 Attach one split ring to each end of each bead link, then attach the hammered links between them.

MAKE AND ATTACH THE CLASP

Make a <u>simple hook and loop clasp</u> and attach it to the necklace.

Variation

As an extra touch, add one or two rows of extra chain to the center of the necklace.

Loopy Loops Necklace

FINISHED SIZE:
20", not including the drop

SKILL LEVEL: Easy

MATERIALS:

- 1" of 14-gauge wire
- 5½" of 18-gauge wire
- 12 feet of 20-gauge wire
- 3 feet of 22-gauge wire
- 25g package of cube-shaped 4mm glass beads
- Mandrel or various-sized round objects
- Needle file or silicon carbide cloth
- Wire cutters
- Chain nose pliers
- Round nose pliers

Bright beads add sparkle to this fun project that lets you practice your wrapping technique.

MAKE THE CHAIN

1 WOTWS, and using the 20-gauge wire, form rings varying in size from ½"-1" in diameter using a mandrel or various-sized round objects, overlapping the ends ¾". Place one, two or three beads on some of the rings, leaving about half of them plain.

2 Link one ring onto another; cut 1" of 22-gauge wire and <u>wrap</u> the center of the ¾" overlap of each. Continue adding links one at a time.

3 Using a round nose pliers, tightly turn the ends into small loops inside the ring.

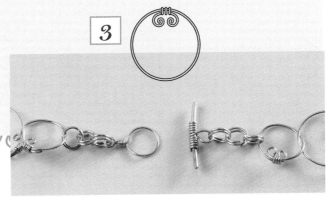

MAKE AND ATTACH THE SPLIT RINGS

1 WOTWS, make six <u>split rings</u> using the 20-gauge wire.

2 Place three split rings on each end of the necklace.

MAKE AND ATTACH THE CLASP

1 Make and attach a <u>toggle clasp</u>.

2 Optional: Attach additional rings to the front of the necklace in any pattern desired.

Beaded Charm Necklace

FINISHED SIZE: 16"

SKILL LEVEL: Easy

MATERIALS:

8 feet of 18-gauge wire

9 assorted 10mm-18mm beads to fit onto 18-gauge wire

15 feet of 1mm tan leather cord

Masking tape

6" of 20-gauge wire

Clasp

Needle file or silicon carbide cloth

Wire cutters

Chain nose pliers

Round nose pliers

Chasing hammer

Anvil

Choose a mixture of glass and porcelain beads. Be sure to attach all of the coils to one side of the braid.

MAKE THE WRAPPED BEAD DROPS

1 Cut nine lengths of 18-gauge wire, each 6".

2 Make nine <u>wrapped bead drops</u>, forming the end of the wire into a large coil; hammer the coil to flatten.

MAKE THE FLAT COIL DROPS

1 Cut eight lengths of 18-gauge wire, each 4½".

2 Make eight <u>flat coil drops</u>.

ASSEMBLE THE NECKLACE

1 Cut the leather cord into six lengths, 30" each.

2 About 5" from one end, tape the leather cords together.

3 Divide the cords into three double strands; braid the doubled strands for about 3", and add on a beaded coil.

4 Braid for approximately ⅜", and add on a plain coil; continue braiding and alternating the beaded with the plain coils ⅜" apart.

5 After the final drop has been added to the necklace, braid for about 3".

6 Adjust the ends until the necklace is 16" in length; tape the braid end.

MAKE AND ATTACH THE CORD ENDS

1 Cut two lengths of 20-gauge wire, each 3".

2 Make a <u>cord end</u> at each end.

MAKE AND ATTACH THE CLASP

1 Make and attach an <u>"S" clasp</u>.

Hammered Drops Necklace

FINISHED SIZE: 16"
SKILL LEVEL: Easy
MATERIALS:

33" of 16-gauge wire
14 turquoise 6mm beads
13 size 11/0 seed beads or other small round beads
2 feet of flexible beading wire
2 crimp beads
16 silver ½" tube beads
30 round silver 2mm beads
5" of 20-gauge wire
Crimping pliers
Needle file or silicon carbide cloth
Chain nose pliers
Round nose pliers
Chasing hammer
Anvil

Turquoise and silver combine to make a simply elegant necklace. String a seed bead or other small bead inside each of the hammered drops so they hang evenly.

MAKE THE HAMMERED DROPS

1 Cut the following lengths from 16-gauge wire:

NAME	QUANTITY	LENGTH
Drop A	4	2"
Drop B	4	2½"
Drop C	5	3"

2 Hammer the pieces flat.

3 Using a round nose pliers, bend the top of each around twice.

MAKE THE WRAPPED BEAD LINKS

1 Cut two lengths of 20-gauge wire, each 2½".

2 Make two wrapped bead links using a tube bead for each.

ASSEMBLE THE NECKLACE

1 Make two wrapped bead links using 20-gauge wire, a 2mm silver bead, a tube bead and a 2mm silver bead for each.

2 Using one crimp bead and the crimping pliers, crimp the beading wire onto one of the wrapped bead links.

3 String 4½" of tube beads alternating with 2mm round beads.

4 String one 6mm turquoise bead followed by a hammered drop; alternate the turquoise beads and drops, using the drops in order of size, smallest to largest; the largest drops should be in the center.

5 String another 4½" of tube beads alternating with 2mm round beads.

6 End the strand by using the other crimp bead and crimping pliers to crimp the beading wire onto the remaining bead link.

MAKE AND ATTACH THE CLASP

1 Make and attach an "S" clasp.

Post Earrings

Clockwise from top: Ball of String, Flat Coil, Hammered Drop.

SKILL LEVEL: Easy

MATERIALS:

- 20- or 21-gauge silver or gold wire
- Beads as desired
- Pair of ear nuts for each pair of earrings
- Needle file and silicon carbide cloth
- Wire cutters
- Chain nose pliers
- Round nose pliers
- Chasing hammer
- Anvil

Note: For any of the following variations, make a second earring to match, and place an ear nut on each.

Post earrings are very simple to make — one backwards bend of the wire creates the post. Make sure the post end is filed and sanded smooth.

FLAT COIL

1 WOTWS, make a <u>flat coil</u>, and hammer the coil.

2 Using a chain nose pliers, turn ⅜" of wire to the back, and cut the wire.

BALL OF STRING

1 WOTWS, coil the wire randomly using a round nose pliers until the bead is about ½" across.

2 Using a chain nose pliers, turn ⅜" of wire to the back, and cut the wire.

HAMMERED DROP

1 Cut 3" of wire.

2 Hammer ¼" of one end.

3 String a bead and shape the wire into a back-and-forth design, and hammer gently.

4 Using a chain nose pliers, turn ⅜" of wire to the back and cut the wire.

Earrings Collection 1

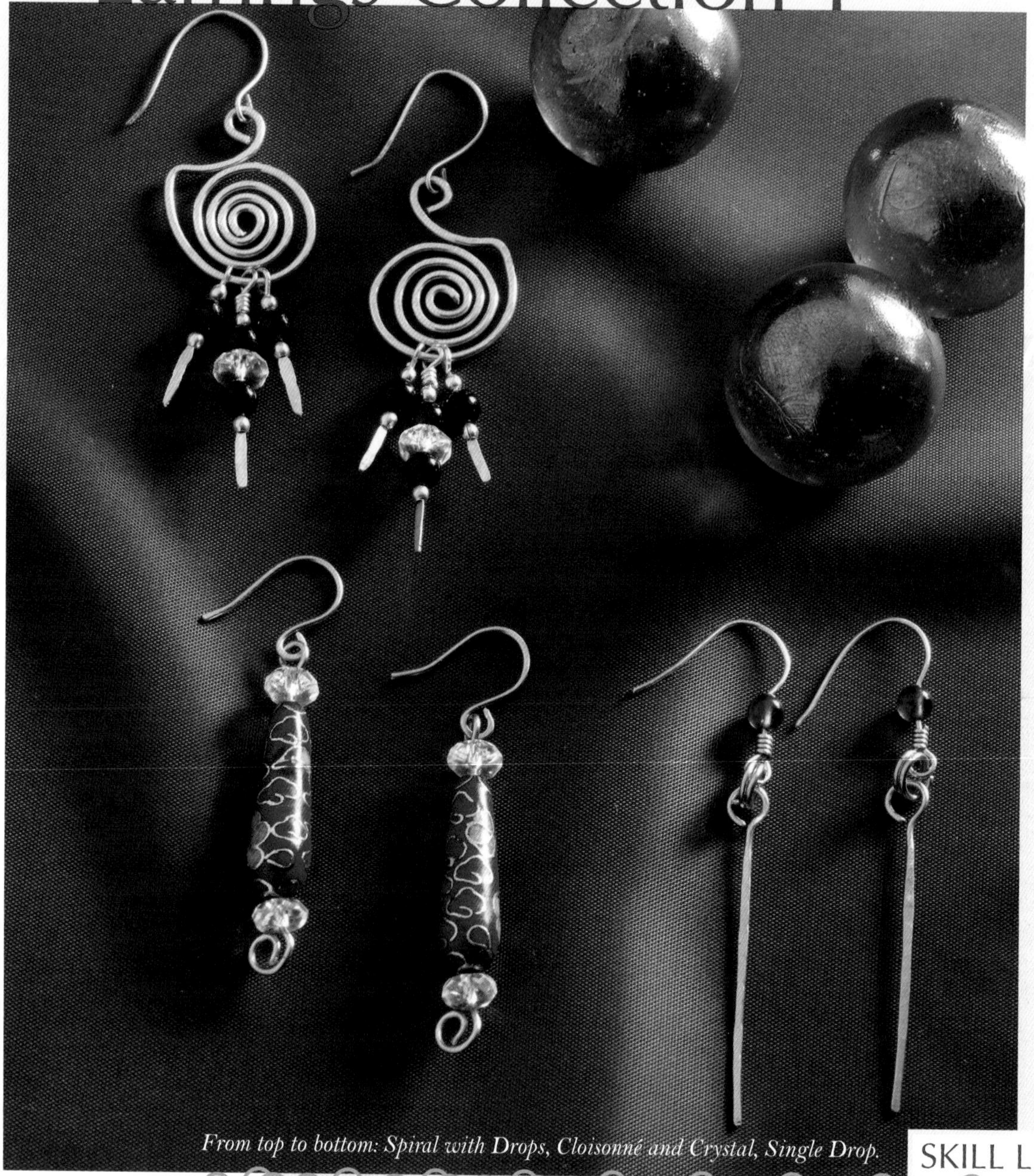

From top to bottom: Spiral with Drops, Cloisonné and Crystal, Single Drop.

SKILL LEVEL: Easy

Collect some pretty beads and create a wardrobe of earrings using basic links and drops. Rather than duplicating the designs shown here, choose beads to go with your wardrobe or your moods.

Single Drop

MATERIALS:

12" of 20-gauge wire

2 amethyst 4mm beads

2 silver coil 2mm beads

Needle file or silicon carbide cloth

Wire cutters

Chain nose pliers

Round nose pliers

Chasing hammer

Anvil

MAKE THE CHAIN

1 Cut 2" of wire.

2 Bend a <u>simple loop</u> at the top; hammer the remainder.

3 Make a <u>split ring</u>; attach it to the simple loop.

4 Make an <u>ear wire</u> using an amethyst and a coil bead; attach it to the split ring.

5 Repeat to make a second earring.

Cloisonné and Crystal

MATERIALS:

4" of 20-gauge wire

2 red cloisonné 22 x 7mm beads

4 disc-shaped crystal 6mm x 3mm beads

Pair of ear wires

Needle file or silicon carbide cloth

Wire cutters

Chain nose pliers

Round nose pliers

MAKE THE EARRINGS

1 Cut 2" of wire.

2 String one cloisonné bead with a crystal bead at each end.

3 Bend a <u>simple loop</u> at the top, and coil the bottom up to the beads.

4 Attach an ear wire to the simple loop.

5 Repeat to make a second earring.

Spiral with Drops

MATERIALS:

12" of 18-gauge wire

10" of 20-gauge wire

8 onyx 4mm beads

2 crystal 3mm x 6mm beads

12 silver 2mm beads

Pair of ear wires

Needle file or silicon carbide cloth

Wire cutters

Chain nose pliers

Round nose pliers

Chasing hammer

Anvil

MAKE THE OPEN COIL

1 Cut 6" of 18-gauge wire.

2 Using a round nose pliers, bend the wire into an open-coil shape.

3 Using a round nose pliers, bend a loop at the top and hammer to flatten.

MAKE AND ATTACH THE SIMPLE BEAD DROPS

1 Make three simple bead drops out of 20-gauge wire and the beads, varying the lengths.

2 Hammer the ends.

3 Attach the drops to the spiral.

4 Attach an ear wire.

5 Repeat to make a second earring.

Endless Chain and Earrings

FINISHED SIZE OF NECKLACE:
42"

FINISHED SIZE OF EARRINGS 1:
3½"

FINISHED SIZE OF EARRINGS 2:
2½"

SKILL LEVEL: Intermediate

MATERIALS:

5½ feet of purchased chain with 2.2mm links

29 faceted 6mm x 3mm crystal beads

4 feet of 22-gauge wire

9" of 18-gauge wire

2" of 21-gauge wire

2 purple 4mm glass beads

14 jump rings

8 silver 2mm round beads

2 pairs of ear wires

Needle file or silicon carbide cloth

Wire cutters

Chain nose pliers

Round nose pliers

Crystal beads appear to float along the fine chain of this necklace. Wrap the chain twice, or wear it long. Graceful chains add pizzazz to two pairs of earrings.

Necklace

1 Cut 15 lengths of chain, each 2¼".

2 Cut 15 lengths of 22-gauge wire, 2" each.

3 Make a <u>wrapped bead link</u> using one crystal bead and one 2" length of wire; fasten one end of the wrapped bead link to one piece of chain, and the other to another piece of chain.

4 Follow Step 3 to make a continuous chain, using a total of 15 wrapped bead links.

Earrings 1

1 Cut one length of chain in each of the following sizes: 1¼", 1½" and 2".

2 Make three <u>wrapped bead links</u> using a crystal bead and a 2mm silver bead for each, fastening each onto a chain length as you make it.

3 Make a wrapped bead link using a 2mm silver bead, fastening one end to the three chains.

4 Attach an ear wire.

5 Repeat to make a second earring.

Earrings 2

1 Cut one 2½" length of 18-gauge wire; bend it according to the shape shown in the diagram.

2 Cut one 2" length of 18-gauge wire; bend it into a <u>coiled drop</u>.

3 Cut one ⅞" length of 21-gauge wire; make a <u>simple bead drop</u> using a 4mm bead and a crystal bead.

4 Fasten the simple bead drop to the bottom of the coil drop.

5 Cut one length of chain in each of the following sizes: 2", 2¼" and 2½".

6 Place a jump ring on each end of each cut piece of chain.

7 Open the end loops slightly of the piece made in Step 1; attach the three chain pieces, with the shortest in the center and the longest at the outside.

8 Fasten the top loop of each coil to the top loop of the first pieces made.

9 Fasten a jump ring to the top and attach it to an ear wire.

10 Repeat to make a second earring.

1

Wired Turquoise Bracelet

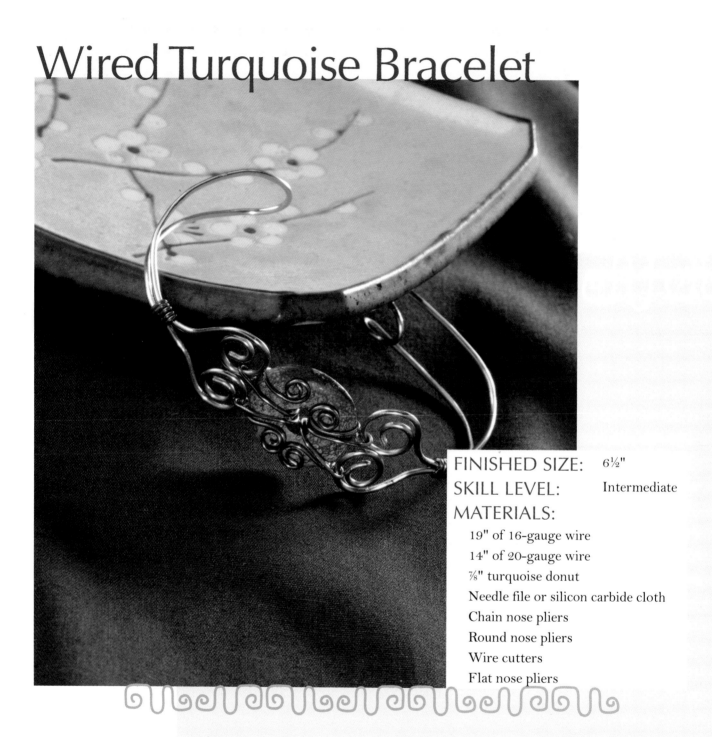

FINISHED SIZE: 6½"
SKILL LEVEL: Intermediate
MATERIALS:

19" of 16-gauge wire

14" of 20-gauge wire

⅞" turquoise donut

Needle file or silicon carbide cloth

Chain nose pliers

Round nose pliers

Wire cutters

Flat nose pliers

For an interesting effect, combine wire colors. This bracelet hinges alongside the donut. Make adjustments to the 16-gauge wire to change the size.

MAKE THE BRACELET

1   Cut 9" of 16-gauge wire; bend it according to the diagram.

2   Cut 10" of 16-gauge wire; bend it according to the diagram, but make the piece ½" longer than the first piece.

3   Cut two lengths of 20-gauge wire, 2" each; <u>wrap</u> one wire around each 16-gauge piece about 1" from the coiled end (see photo at left).

4   Cut four 2½" lengths of 20-gauge wire; one at a time, bend one end into a small loop and fasten it to one of the coiled ends. Wrap the wire down through the donut hole, then bring it up to the front and bend a coil.

5   Bend the longer 16-gauge wire piece ½" from the end to form a clasp. Shape the bracelet to fit your wrist.

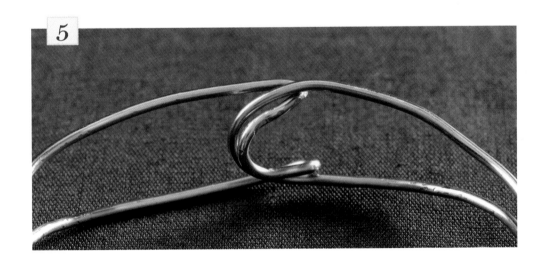

Crystal Rose Pendant

FINISHED SIZE: 17"

SKILL LEVEL: Intermediate

MATERIALS:

11" of 14-gauge silver wire

5 light blue faceted crystal 4mm beads

10" of 22-gauge silver wire

6" of 18-gauge gold wire

30" of 18-gauge silver wire

20-gauge silver wire

Clasp

Needle file or silicon carbide cloth

Wire cutters

Chain nose pliers

Round nose pliers

Flat nose pliers

Chasing hammer

Anvil

Simple bending with wired-on crystal beads
makes a dramatic pendant.

MAKE THE PENDANT

1 With 14-gauge wire and WOTWS, begin at the center of the rose shape and bend a loop.

2 Form the wire into a rose-like shape, ending with a loop for hanging, using either a round nose or chain nose pliers, and cut the wire. Hammer.

3 Cut 2" of 22-gauge wire and wrap it two or three times around a part of the rose piece; string a crystal bead, and wrap again to fasten. Repeat for all crystal beads.

4 WOTWS and with the gold wire, bend a leaf shape as shown in the diagram.

5 Hammer the leaf shape.

6 Fasten the leaf shape securely onto the rose by bending it at the top with a chain nose pliers.

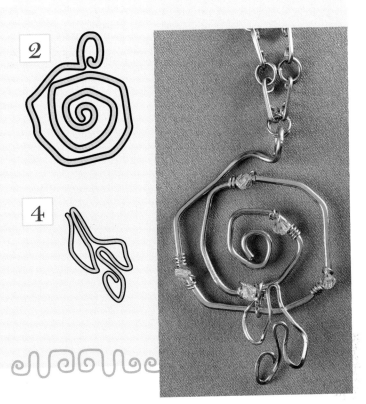

MAKE THE CHAIN

1 Cut 30 lengths of 18-gauge wire, each 1".

2 Make a <u>hammered link chain</u>, making 30 links out of the 1" lengths.

3 Make a <u>split ring</u> to go between (and attach) each of the links.

4 Attach the pendant to the center split ring of the chain.

5 Attach a clasp.

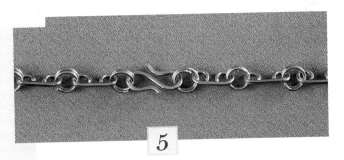

Pewter Beads Bracelet

FINISHED SIZE: 7"

SKILL LEVEL: Intermediate

MATERIALS:

  3 feet of 18-gauge wire

  16" of 20-gauge wire

  12 tube-shape 10mm x 6mm pewter beads

  24 cube 4mm seed beads

  Needle file or silicon carbide cloth

  Wire cutters

  Chain nose pliers

  Round nose pliers

  Flat nose pliers

Once you begin this bracelet, you may find it simpler than it looks!

MAKE THE BRACELET

1 Cut two lengths of 18-gauge wire, each 18". Bend the wires in half and place one inside the other to make the looped end of the bracelet. Bring all of the wires together about 1" from the outer bend, keeping them flat.

2 Cut 2" of 20-gauge wire; <u>wrap</u> it 1" from the bend.

3 Pull the two outer wires outward and string one seed bead, one pewter bead, and one seed bead onto each; bring the wires together.

4 Cut seven lengths of 20-gauge wire, 2" each; wrap after the beads and repeat to make six beaded sections.

5 Wrap after the final beaded section, then trim the two outer wires to ¾".

6 Bend each end into a loop to the sides.

7 Trim the two inner wires to 1", bend the ends sharply inwards, then form a clasp shape, as shown in the photo at left.

1-2

Beaded Cuff

FINISHED SIZE: 6"

SKILL LEVEL: Intermediate

MATERIALS:

  15" of 14-gauge wire

  6 feet of 24-gauge coated craft wire

  Assorted 11/0 seed beads

  Assorted 4mm beads

  Round object (like a coffee mug)

  Needle file or silicon carbide cloth

  Wire cutters

  Chain nose pliers

  Round nose pliers

Make a comfortable cuff bracelet out of wire with randomly woven strands of beads. Finish it with a picot edging.

MAKE THE BRACELET BASE

1. Grasp the center of the 14-gauge wire with a round nose pliers, bend in half, then shape the cuff making a small coil at each end.

2. Bend the piece over a rounded object such as a coffee mug, then bend to fit your arm.

3. Cut 18" of 24-gauge wire; wrap one end tightly four or five times around the cuff wire, string some seed beads intermixed with 4mm beads, enough to go from one side to the other, then wrap again at the other side of the cuff.

4. String more beads, wrap at the other side, and continue to do this from one end to the other. Once finished, turn around and go back.

5. Randomly weave the new strands through the originally placed strands. Continue until the cuff is as covered as you want it to be, adding new lengths of wire as needed.

MAKE THE PICOT EDGING

1. Fasten 18" of 24-gauge wire to the bracelet base.

2. String a short sequence of seed beads, then form the beads into a "U" shape, and wrap.

3. Continue stringing beads and wrapping until the edges are complete.

Feather Key Ring

FINISHED SIZE: 5"
SKILL LEVEL: Intermediate
MATERIALS:

9" of 14-gauge wire
14" of 18-gauge wire
Small pieces of assorted leather cords
32mm bone donut
Assortment of glass, pewter and silver beads to fit
Feather
1"-diameter dowel
Needle file or silicon carbide cloth
Wire cutters
Round nose pliers
Chain nose pliers

Key rings are a great way to use up stash leftovers — those pieces that haven't worked themselves into other jewelry. Add some feathers!

MAKE THE KEY RING

1 WOTWS, wrap the 14-gauge wire around a 1" diameter dowel twice so it is doubled throughout (due to the density of the wire, the ring may turn out to be slightly larger than 1").

2 Cut one length of leather cord in each of the following lengths: 4" and 3½".

3 String the beads of your choice onto each leather strand; tie a knot to hold the beads in place.

4 Cut 8" of leather cord; tie a <u>lark's head knot</u> onto the donut.

5 Cut 6" of 18-gauge wire.

6 Make a <u>flat coil</u>, leaving 1¼". Bend the end around the donut.

7 Bring the leather cords and the feather together and temorarily bind using masking tape.

8 Cut 4" of 18-gauge wire and make a <u>cord end</u> to attach the feather and leather cords.

Crocheted Chain Bracelet

FINISHED SIZE: 7½"

SKILL LEVEL: Intermediate

MATERIALS:

10 yd. 28-gauge coated craft wire

Size D crochet hook

12" of 20-gauge wire

Your choice of bead(s) to make a charm

Needle file or silicon carbide cloth

Wire cutters

Chain nose pliers

Round nose pliers

A crocheted chain makes a simple but stunning statement.

MAKE THE CROCHETED CHAIN

1. Make a crocheted chain 27" long out of the coated craft wire.

2. Tie the ends together to make the chain continuous; keep the knot at one end and fold the piece until it is four strands thick.

3. Cut 3" of 20-gauge wire.

4. Bend a loop at the center of the wire; place one end of the crocheted strands onto it, then crisscross the wire.

5. Form a wrapped loop for the clasp catch with one end, and wrap the crocheted strands with the other.

6. Cut 3½" of 20-gauge wire.

7. Bend a loop 2" from one end, catching the other end of the crocheted strands; crisscross the wire and form the long end into a clasp hook.

8. Finish the end by wrapping it.

9. Wrap the short end around the crocheted strands.

MAKE THE WRAPPED BEAD DROP

Cut a length of 20-gauge wire the length of the bead or beads plus 2"; make a wrapped bead drop, fastening it onto the bracelet.

Crocheted Chain Necklace

FINISHED SIZE: 21"

SKILL LEVEL: Intermediate

MATERIALS:

2 feet of 18-gauge wire

15 yd. 28-gauge colored wire

Size D crochet hook

3 dozen assorted glass beads

Clasp

Needle file or silicon carbide cloth

Wire cutters

Chain nose pliers

Round nose pliers

The airy look of a crocheted chain is accented by light-catching glass beads.

MAKE THE SIMPLE BEAD LINKS

Make <u>simple bead links</u> using the glass beads and the 18-gauge wire to make two strands, each 3½" long.

MAKE THE CROCHETED CHAIN

1 WOTWS, string the remaining beads onto the 28-gauge wire and begin a <u>crocheted chain</u>.

2 At random intervals, slide a bead up to the hook, pull on the loop on the hook until the loop is the length of the bead, then complete the chain stitch; continue until the strand is 102" long.

3 Cut the wire, leaving an end about 3" long.

4 Pull the final chain stitch tight, tie the two ends of the wire together, and work the loose ends into the strand.

5 Fold the piece until it is eight strands thick, keeping the knot at one end.

6 Cut two 1" lengths of 18-gauge wire.

7 Make a small loop at one end of the 1" length, catching one end of the folded strands into it.

MAKE AND ATTACH THE END CAP

1 WOTWS and using 18-gauge wire, make an <u>end cap</u>.

2 Place the end cap over the loop made in Step 7.

3 Bend the remaining end of the 1" wire into a loop, and repeat to finish the other end.

4 Attach one bead link strand to each end loop.

5 Attach a clasp.

Pearls with Fancy Clasp and Earrings

FINISHED SIZE OF NECKLACE:	16"
FINISHED SIZE OF EARRINGS:	1¾"
SKILL LEVEL:	Intermediate

MATERIALS:

16" strand of 6mm round pearls

11 square ⅝" shell beads, drilled through the center

4 feet of white nylon or silk bead cord

Flexible beading needle

2 bead tips

18" of 20-gauge wire

5" of 22-gauge wire

Masking tape

Clear nail polish

Beading tweezers

Pair of ear wires

⅜"-diameter dowel

Needle file or silicon carbide cloth

Wire cutters

Chain nose or flat nose pliers

Round nose pliers

Chasing hammer

Anvil

Pearls and shells go together naturally, a peaceful blending of subtle shades and textures. Add an elegant finishing touch with a fancy wire clasp.

Necklace

MAKE THE KNOTTED STRAND

1 Line up 15" of beads, placing 22 pearls along each side, and seven shell beads alternating with pearls in the center.

2 Make a <u>knotted strand using bead tips</u>.

MAKE AND ATTACH THE CLASP

1 Cut two 3" lengths of 20-gauge wire. Form the center of each around a ⅜" dowel. <u>Coil</u> the ends and hammer the pieces gently.

2 Cut 2½" of wire. <u>Coil</u> 1" of one end. Hammer the coil gently and form the remaining end into a loop.

3 Cut 3" of wire. Form the same as Step 2, making the end loop longer.

4 Assemble the two wire pieces for each half of the clasp as shown, and tape together.

5 Cut 1¼" of 22-gauge wire. Wrap the wire at the base of the loop made in Step 2.

6 Cut 2" of 22-gauge wire. <u>Wrap</u> the wire at the center

7 Repeat Steps 5-6 for the second half of the clasp.

8 Shape the longer loop into a hook, and fasten a bead tip onto each clasp piece.

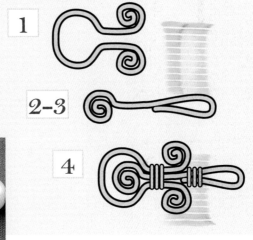

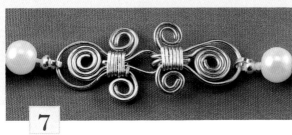

Earrings

1 Cut 20-gauge wire the length of three pearls and two shell beads, plus 1¼".

2 Make a <u>wrapped bead drop</u>, alternating the pearls and shells.

3 Hammer ¼" of the lower end of the drop.

4 Attach the top loop to an ear wire.

5 Repeat to make a second earring.

Tube Bead Bracelet

FINISHED SIZE: 8"

SKILL LEVEL: Intermediate

MATERIALS:

  11/0 Delica seed beads

  Size D nylon beading thread

  12" of 16-gauge wire

  Needle file or silicon carbide cloth

  Beading needle

  Round nose pliers

  Chasing hammer

  Anvil

To make this sleek bracelet, choose five related bead colors and change colors every two rows for a subtly shaded effect.

MAKE THE BRACELET

1 Follow the <u>peyote tube bead</u> instructions, beginning with 140 beads (this makes a tube approx. 7⅜" long) and work for ten rows, then join.

2 Carefully slide the 16-gauge wire into the beaded tube and bend into a bracelet shape.

3 Arrange the wire so 1" shows at one end of the tube. Bend the tip tightly to one side, and hammer to flatten, then bend sharply at the end of the tube and form a clasp.

4 Hammer the remaining end, bend sharply at the end of the tube, form a loop, wrap at the base of the loop and then decoratively around the tube taking care to not damage the beading.

Earrings Collection 2

From top to bottom: Aventurine Drops, Peridot Hoops and Wired Pearls.

SKILL LEVEL: Intermediate

Use a variety of wiring techniques including jig shapes, hoops and wrapping to make some charming earrings.

Aventurine Drops

MATERIALS:

25" of 20-gauge wire

10 green aventurine 4mm-6mm pebble beads

Jig

Pair of ear wires

Needle file or silicon carbide cloth

Wire cutters

Chain nose or flat nose pliers

Round nose pliers

Chasing hammer

Anvil

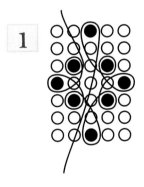

MAKE THE EARRINGS

1 Cut 8" of 20-gauge wire and begin forming the jig shape 1" from one end according to the diagram. Remove from the jig and hammer gently to set the loops.

2 <u>Wrap</u> the 1" end just beneath the top loop of the jig piece.

3 Place two beads onto the long end of the wire, and wrap the wire end around the lower loop of the jig piece.

4 Make three <u>wrapped bead drops</u> with hammered ends and using one pebble bead for each and place onto three loops of the jig piece.

5 Attach an ear wire.

6 Repeat to make a second earring.

Peridot Hoops

MATERIALS:

18" of 18-gauge wire

24" of 22-gauge wire

3½" of 20-gauge wire

26 peridot 4mm crystal beads

2 crystal 9mm x 15mm beads

Pair of ear wires

Needle file or silicon carbide cloth

Wire cutters

Chain nose or flat nose pliers

Round nose pliers

Round form, such as a nail polish bottle

MAKE THE EARRINGS

1 WOTWS, wrap 18-gauge wire twice around a round form such as a small bottle to make a 1¼" hoop, overlapping the ends ½".

2 Cut 12" of 22-gauge wire; fasten ½" from one end of the hoop and wrap two or three times.

3 String on a peridot crystal bead, and wrap after the bead.

4 Continue around, adding on 12 beads in all; trim any excess wire.

5 Finish the hoop by bending a loop in each end, facing one upwards and one downwards.

6 Make a <u>simple bead drop</u> out of 20-gauge wire using the large crystal and one peridot bead. Fasten it to the downward facing loop.

7 Attach an ear wire.

8 Repeat to make a second earring.

Wired Pearls

MATERIALS:

10" of 18-gauge wire

12" of 22-gauge wire

12 pearl 4mm beads

Jig

Pair of ear wires

Needle file or silicon carbide cloth

Wire cutters

Round nose pliers

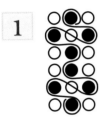

MAKE THE EARRINGS

1 Cut 5" of 18-gauge wire and shape the wire on the jig according to the diagram.

2 Cut 6" of 22-gauge wire and <u>wrap</u> two or three times under the topmost loop of the jig piece.

3 String on a pearl, and wrap beneath it.

4 Continue to string on a pearl at a time and wrap for the length of the jig piece.

5 Attach an ear wire.

6 Repeat to make a second earring.

Twists and Braids Cuff

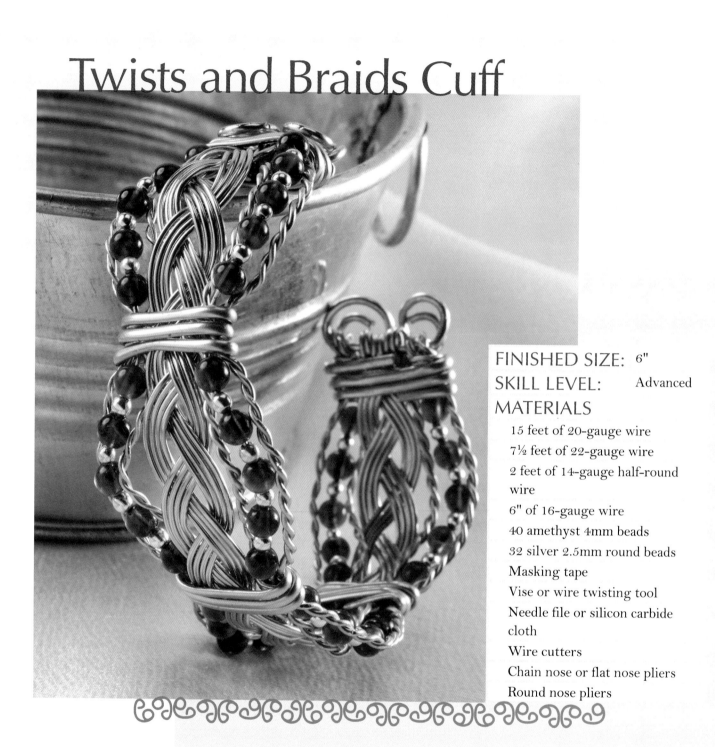

FINISHED SIZE: 6"
SKILL LEVEL: Advanced
MATERIALS

15 feet of 20-gauge wire
7½ feet of 22-gauge wire
2 feet of 14-gauge half-round wire
6" of 16-gauge wire
40 amethyst 4mm beads
32 silver 2.5mm round beads
Masking tape
Vise or wire twisting tool
Needle file or silicon carbide cloth
Wire cutters
Chain nose or flat nose pliers
Round nose pliers

Accept this piece as a challenge to your skills — three sections are combined to make the width. The sections made individually will also make lovely bracelets.

MAKE THE OUTER BEADED SECTIONS

1 Cut four 10" lengths of 20-gauge wire. Place two together and fasten in a vise and twist. Repeat using the remaining two lengths.

2 Cut 10" of 22-gauge wire. Center it between the two twisted wires, and securely tape 1" from one end.

3 Pull the twisted wires to each side of the 22-gauge wire and place five amethyst beads alternating with silver beads onto the 22-gauge wire.

4 Bend the twisted wires around the beads.

5 Cut 1¼" of 22-gauge wire and wrap just past the beaded section.

6 Repeat Steps 3-5 to make four beaded sections.

7 Carefully shape each beaded section so it bends outward (see photo).

8 Repeat Steps 1-7 to make a second section.

MAKE THE BRAIDED SECTION

1 Cut 3" of 16-gauge wire.

2 Cut six 16" lengths of 20-gauge wire. Bend them in half over the 16-gauge wire.

3 Bend back the ends of the 16-gauge wire and place in a vise. Divide the 20-gauge wires into groups of four, and braid for 6".

4 Trim the ends evenly, leaving about ⅜" beyond the braid, and wrap the ends one at a time around a 3" length of 16-gauge wire.

5 Trim the ends of the twisted wires (but do not trim the 22-gauge beaded wire). Wrap them over the 16-gauge wire at one end, placing one twisted wire section on each side of the braided piece.

6 Wrap the 22-gauge wire around the sections several times and trim. Repeat for the other end.

FINISH THE CUFF

1 Using the 14-gauge half-round wire, make <u>wraps</u> between each beaded section and at the ends, bringing the wires snugly together.

2 <u>Coil</u> the ends of the 16-gauge wires.

3 Gently shape the cuff to fit your wrist.

Chandelier
Pendant and Earrings

FINISHED SIZE OF NECKLACE:
24"

FINISHED SIZE OF EARRINGS:
3"

SKILL LEVEL: Advanced

MATERIALS

2½ feet of 18-gauge wire

8 feet of 20-gauge wire

4" of 22-gauge wire

19 "pearl" 3mm beads

19 crystal 6mm x 3mm beads

Jig

Masking tape

Clasp

Pair of ear wires

Needle file or silicon carbide cloth

Wire cutters

Chain nose nose pliers

Round nose pliers

Chasing hammer

Anvil

Assembled wrapped shapes make an intricate-looking pendant. Soft pearls and hammered drops add a decadent touch.

Necklace

MAKE THE PENDANT

1 WOTWS and using 18-gauge wire, shape the wire on the jig according to the diagram.

2 Cut 2¾" of 18-gauge wire. Bend the center shape in the diagram using a round nose pliers.

3 Cut 1¾" of 18-gauge wire. Bend the topmost shape in the diagram using a round nose pliers.

4 Align the pieces and tape them together.

5 Cut three lengths of 22-gauge wire, each 1¼". Make three <u>wraps</u> to fasten the shapes together, and hammer gently to set the piece.

6 Cut two lengths of 20-gauge wire, each 1". Make <u>simple bead links</u> using a 3mm pearl bead for each. Fasten the simple bead links to the top loops of the pendant.

7 Cut seven lengths of 20-gauge wire, each 1½". For each: bend a loop at the bottom; string a crystal bead and a 3mm bead, and bend a loop at the top.

8 Attach one drop to each of the seven loops of the jig piece.

9 Cut seven lengths of 20-gauge wire, each 1". Bend a loop at the top of each, hammer the remainder, and attach one to each drop.

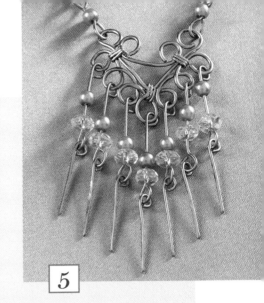

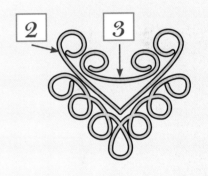

MAKE THE CHAIN

1 Cut 46 lengths of 20-gauge wire, each 1". Hammer the center of each.

2 Make two lengths of <u>simple chain</u>; fasten one to each simple bead link.

3 Attach a clasp.

Earrings

1 WOTWS, shape the wire on the jig according to the diagram leaving an end about ¼" long.

2 Hammer the piece gently, then bend the ¼" end over the wire to the back.

3 Follow Steps 7-9 above to make and attach five links and five drops.

4 Attach an ear wire.

5 Repeat to make a second earring.

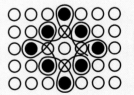

Circle and Fan Pendant

FINISHED SIZE: 20"

SKILL LEVEL: Advanced

MATERIALS:

10" of 18-gauge wire

3" of 16-gauge half-round wire

7 feet of 20-gauge wire

4 feet of 22-gauge wire

⅞" x ⅜" fancy red bead

Clasp

1" diameter round object

Needle file or silicon carbide cloth

Wire cutters

Chain nose pliers

Round nose pliers

Flat nose pliers

Chasing hammer

Anvil

Showcase a pretty bead by combining it with an interesting wire piece. The chain is a wrapped variation of eyelet chain.

MAKE THE PENDANT

1. WOTWS, wrap the 18-gauge wire around a 1" diameter round object twice, overlapping the ends. Cut, allowing ½" for a simple loop at one end, and 1" for wrapping at the other end.

2. Bend the <u>simple loop</u>, and wrap the other end around the ring just past the loop.

3. Cut 1¼" of the half-round wire. <u>Wrap</u> it around one side of the ring three times, and repeat on the other side.

4. Cut three lengths of 20-gauge wire, each 2½". Hammer to flatten. Center one length diagonally on the ring, wrap each end once tightly, and then squeeze the wrap with pliers. Repeat for the remaining two wires, placing them in a fan-like formation.

5. Make a <u>simple bead link</u> using the fancy bead and 20-gauge wire.

6. Cut 20-gauge wire in three varying lengths between 1½" and 1¼". Turn the top of each into a loop and hammer the remainder. Fasten the lengths to the bottom of the simple bead link, then fasten the bead link onto the ring.

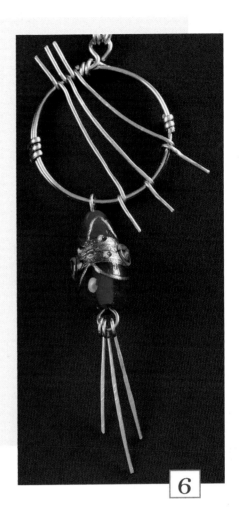

6

MAKE THE CHAIN

1. Cut 38 lengths of 20-gauge wire, each 1¾". Make an <u>eyelet chain</u>, making the loop small (I used the handle of a needle file).

2. Cut 38 lengths of 22-gauge wire, each 1". Wrap the wire just beneath the loop of each link of the chain.

3. Bend the link ends under to form a loop, fastening onto the round loop of the previous link.

4. Make two lengths of chain, fastening each to the top loop of the ring.

5. Attach a clasp.

5

93

Freeform Cuff

FINISHED SIZE: 7¼"

SKILL LEVEL: Advanced

MATERIALS:

18" of 14-gauge wire

18" of 14- or 16-gauge wire

2½ feet of 22-gauge wire

Needle file or silicon carbide cloth

Wire cutters

Flat nose pliers

Round nose pliers

Express your most artful self in creating this free-bent cuff.

MAKE THE FREEFORM DESIGN

1 Cut three lengths of 14-or 16-gauge wire, each 6".

2 Using a round nose pliers, bend each into a freeform design similar to the diagram.

MAKE THE OUTER EDGE OF THE CUFF

1 Bend the 18" of 14-gauge wire in half.

2 Form the cuff to fit around the 6" bent pieces, adding additional shaping as you like.

3 Cut 2" lengths of 22-gauge wire, and <u>wrap</u> at intervals to fasten the shaped piece to the cuff.

4 To finish, curl the ends of the cuff and shape it over a rounded object, then fit it to your wrist.

Tasseled Pendant

FINISHED SIZE: 20"

SKILL LEVEL: Advanced

MATERIALS:

5 feet of 18-gauge wire

2" of 22-gauge wire

3 feet of 20-gauge wire

8" of 16-gauge half-round wire

3 assorted 6mm beads that will fit onto 18-gauge

Rayon embroidery thread

Clasp

Masking tape

3" piece of cardboard

Needle file or silicon carbide cloth

Wire cutters

Chain nose pliers

Flat nose pliers

Round nose pliers

Chasing hammer

Anvil

Finish this elegant pendant with a graceful tassel.

MAKE THE PENDANT

1 Cut five lengths of 18-gauge wire, each 3".

2 String three beads onto one length; shape the remaining four according to the diagram.

3 Tape the pieces together and <u>wrap</u> in five places using the half-round wire, wrapping two or three times for each wrap (see photo for placement).

4 Bend a top and bottom loop in the center wire.

5 Wrap the rayon thread around a 3" piece of cardboard.

6 Cut 1" of 22-gauge wire; place it through the top of the wrappings. Twist to fasten and form the ends into a loop.

7 Cut the bottom of the wrappings. Wrap a short length of 22-gauge wire around the tassel about ⅜" below the top.

MAKE THE CHAIN

1 Cut 32 lengths of 18-gauge wire, each 1¼".

2 Make 18 <u>split rings</u> out of 20-gauge wire;

3 Make two lengths of <u>hammered link chain</u> beginning each at one of the upper loops of the pendant.

4 Attach a clasp.

Butterfly Pendant

FINISHED SIZE: *22"*

SKILL LEVEL: Advanced

MATERIALS:

6 feet of 18-gauge wire

6 feet of 20-gauge wire

2 feet of 22-gauge wire

Large 20mm x 13mm bead

Needle file or silicon carbide cloth

Wire cutters

Chain nose pliers

Flat nose pliers

Round nose pliers

Chasing hammer

Anvil

Twisting tool

Vise

Combine individual pieces by wrapping to create shapes such as this butterfly.

MAKE THE BUTTERFLY PENDANT

1 WOTWS, follow the diagram to make the parts indicated using a round nose pliers, then hammer each piece to flatten slightly.

2 Assemble the pieces and <u>wrap</u> as shown in the photo, using 1¼" lengths of 22-gauge wire. Hammer lightly to set the wraps.

3 Cut two lengths of 20-gauge wire, each 8". Twist them together to make the body. Shape the body as shown in the diagram and wire the body to the wings.

4 Cut a length of 22-gauge wire the length of the bead plus 2". Run the wire through the bead. Place it on the twisted piece and wrap above and below the bead.

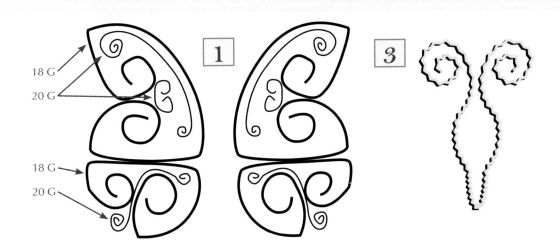

18 G
20 G
18 G
20 G

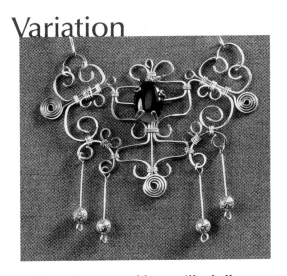

MAKE THE CHAIN

1 Cut 24 lengths of 18-gauge wire, each 1¼".

2 Make 26 <u>split rings</u> out of the 20-gauge wire.

3 Make two <u>hammered link chains</u>.

4 Attach the chains to the loops of the antenna.

5 Attach a clasp.

Variation

This filigree necklace will challenge your wire wrapping and bending skills.

Rippling Waters Cuff

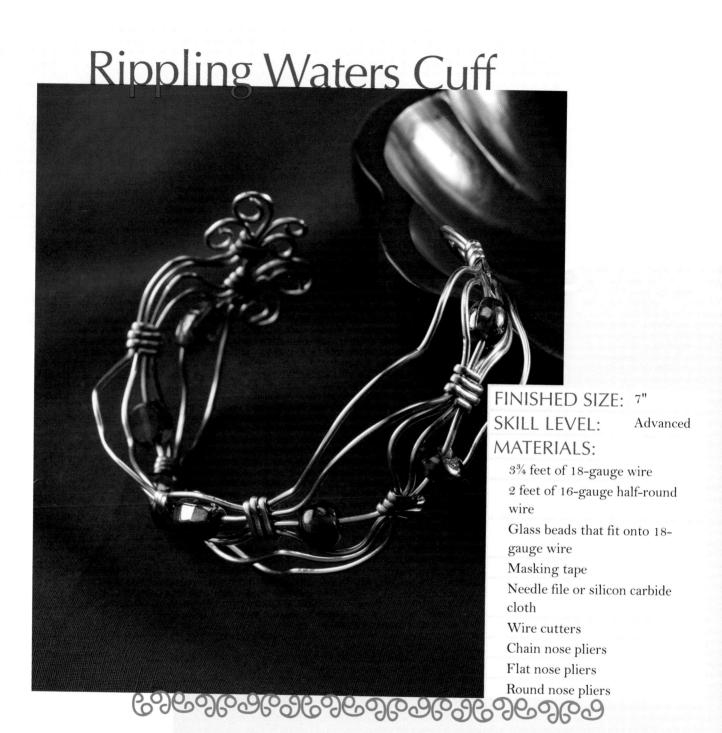

FINISHED SIZE: 7"

SKILL LEVEL: Advanced

MATERIALS:

3¾ feet of 18-gauge wire

2 feet of 16-gauge half-round wire

Glass beads that fit onto 18-gauge wire

Masking tape

Needle file or silicon carbide cloth

Wire cutters

Chain nose pliers

Flat nose pliers

Round nose pliers

The fluid look of this piece is like the motion of water swirling around rocks.

MAKE THE CUFF

1 Cut three lengths of 18-gauge wire, each 15".

2 Hold the wires together and bend a loop at the middle using a round nose pliers, making six strands.

3 Tape four of the wires together. <u>Wrap</u> them three times using the half-round wire.

4 Place one bead on one of the four wires, and bend three of the original four wires plus one other to form around the bead.

5 Wrap below the bead with the half-round wire.

6 Continue to add beads and wrap, choosing which four of the wires to use each time.

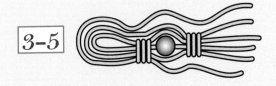

FINISH THE CUFF

1 To end the piece, make two wraps near the end. Trim the ends (if necessary) and bend the wire ends into curls.

2 Shape the cuff to fit your arm.

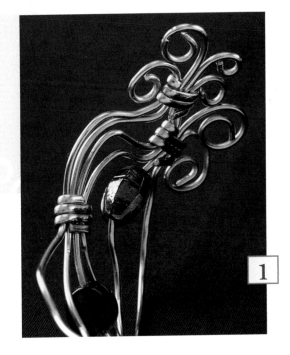

Elegant Neck Ring

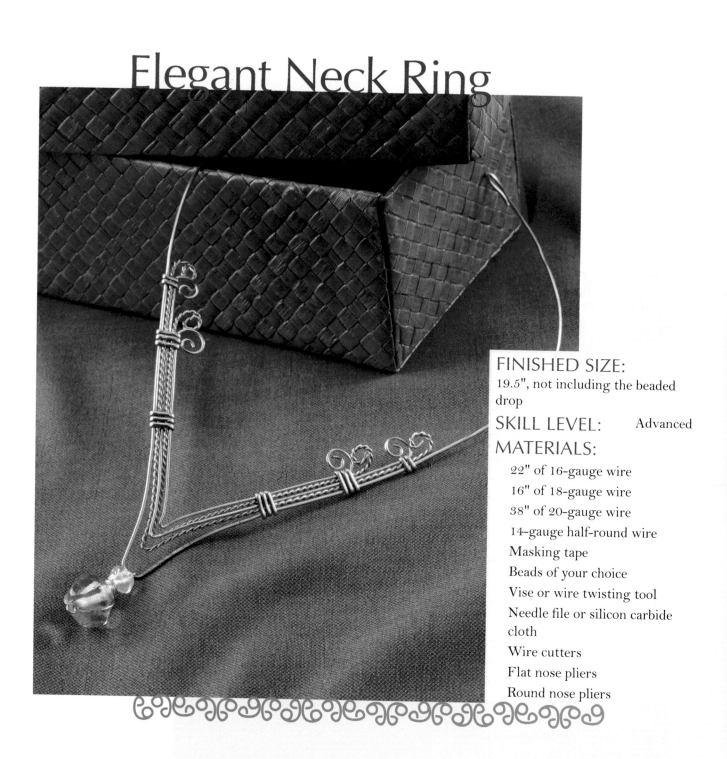

FINISHED SIZE:
19.5", not including the beaded drop

SKILL LEVEL: Advanced

MATERIALS:

22" of 16-gauge wire

16" of 18-gauge wire

38" of 20-gauge wire

14-gauge half-round wire

Masking tape

Beads of your choice

Vise or wire twisting tool

Needle file or silicon carbide cloth

Wire cutters

Flat nose pliers

Round nose pliers

Ply twisted and plain wires for an appealing texture and sculptural quality.

MAKE THE NECK RING

1 Cut a 9" length and 7" length of 18-gauge wire. Set aside.

2 Cut two lengths of 20-gauge wire, each 10". Place the wires in a vise and twist them together.

3 Cut two lengths of 20-gauge wire, each 8". Place the wires in a vise and twist them together.

4 Shape the neck wire by gripping the center of the 16-gauge wire with a chain nose pliers and bending sharply upwards; shape the sides curving gently outward.

5 Bend each of the remaining wires (7"; 8" twisted; 9"; 10" twisted) sharply in the centers. Work the wires carefully to shape them to fit alongside the neck ring, from the longest to the shortest (see photo for placement). Place tape in several places to hold them all in place.

6 Bend 1" of the ends of the 18-gauge and twisted wires into curls.

7 WOTWS, <u>wrap</u> the half-round wire beneath each pair of curls and once more on each side halfway to the center.

8 Shape the back of the neck ring and bend the ends into hook and loop shapes.

MAKE THE SIMPLE BEAD DROP

1 Make a <u>simple bead drop</u> using the beads of your choice.

2 Attach it to the front of the neck ring.

Variations

Make a simple version of this necklace by forming a plain ring and adding a drop pendant, or shape the ends into a fancy clasp that acts as the focal point.

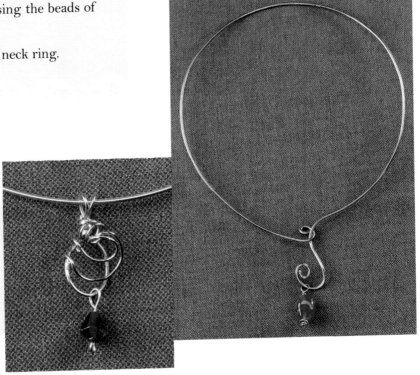

Ring Collection

Make fingers-full of rings! When trying a new design, make the ring first in practice wire and adjust the wire length as needed to make your size. Glass beads may be used in rings, although metal beads such as silver, pewter or cloisonné are sturdier.

Plain Wire Ring

SKILL LEVEL: Easy

MATERIALS:

6" - 7" of 16-gauge wire

Mandrel

Needle file or silicon carbide cloth

Wire cutters

Flat nose pliers

Round nose pliers

MAKE THE RING

1 Wrap the wire around a mandrel.

2 Coil the ends as desired using a round nose pliers.

3 Add <u>wraps</u> to the upper sides if needed.

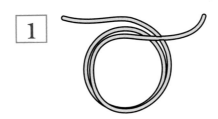

Two-Bead Adjustable Ring

SKILL LEVEL: Advanced

MATERIALS:

15" of 18-gauge wire

6" of 16-gauge half-round wire

2 beads that fit onto 18-gauge wire

Mandrel

Needle file or silicon carbide cloth

Wire cutters

Flat nose pliers

Round nose pliers

MAKE THE RING

1 Cut three lengths of 18-gauge wire, each 5". <u>Wrap</u> using 16-gauge half-round wire about 1½" apart.

2 Form the wires around a mandrel.

3 Separate the wires at each end and string a bead on each center wire.

4 Bring the wires around the beads and wrap again.

5 Finish by bending each wire end into a loop.

Coral and Turquoise Necklace

FINISHED SIZE: 24"

SKILL LEVEL: Advanced

MATERIALS:

16" strand of small coral chip beads

16" strand of 4mm red Howlite beads

16" strand of 2mm x 4mm turquoise tube beads

6 feet of size 1 black beading cord

Flexible beading needle

2 lengths (¼") of silver Bullion (French coil)

15" of 20-gauge wire

1¼" of 22-gauge wire

20mm turquoise donut

Clasp

Needle file or silicon carbide cloth

Wire cutters

Chain nose pliers

Flat nose pliers

Round nose pliers

The rich colors of turquoise and coral enhance a denim shirt as easily as they charm a silk blouse.

PREPARE THE NECKLACE

1 Cut two lengths of 20-gauge wire, each 2¼". Make two <u>wrapped bead links</u> using a 4mm Howlite bead for each.

2 Line up 22" of beads in the following sequence: six coral, one 4mm Howlite, one turquoise tube, and one 4mm Howlite. Repeat for the length of the necklace, placing four turquoise beads at the center to make a place for the bail, and beginning and ending the necklace with three 4mm beads.

MAKE THE KNOTTED STRAND

1 Make a <u>knotted strand using bullion</u>, knotting before and after each section of coral beads (instead of after each bead).

2 Attach a clasp.

ATTACH THE DONUT

1 Cut 7" of 20-gauge wire. Form a <u>lark's head knot</u> onto the donut.

2 Bend the wires above the donut to form a bail.

3 Cut 1¼" of 22-gauge wire and <u>wrap</u> below the bail around all four wires.

4 Curl the wire ends decoratively over the donut.

5 Cut 2½" of 20-gauge wire. Bend the center into a curve and place the bail of the donut onto it.

6 Bend each end snugly around the necklace center to hold the piece in place. Curl the wire ends.

Western-Style Bracelet

FINISHED SIZE: 7¾"

SKILL LEVEL: Advanced

MATERIALS:

30" of 18-gauge wire

18" of 20-gauge wire

10" of 22-gauge wire

Masking tape

Strand of 6-8mm Pietersite pebble beads

2 fancy 6mm silver beads

36 round 2.5mm silver beads

Flexible beading wire

4 crimp beads

Crimping pliers

Clasp

Vise or wire twisting tool

Jig

Needle file or silicon carbide cloth

Wire cutters

Chain nose pliers

Flat nose pliers

Round nose pliers

Dowel

The stringing, jigwork, twisted wire and wrapping give this bracelet its Western flair.

MAKE THE JIG SHAPES

1   Cut six lengths of 18-gauge wire, each 4¼".

2   Form each link on a jig according to the diagram. Bend the ends into loops using a round nose pliers.

3   Cut six lengths of 20-gauge wire, each 2". Place two together in a vise and twist, leaving ½" at each end untwisted, and repeat with the other wires to make three twisted pieces.

4   Align two jig shapes, placing a twisted wire in the center (see photo for placement; tape to hold them butted together (not overlapped). <u>Wrap</u> at each end using 1¼" lengths of 22-gauge wire. Repeat to make three sections. Bend the unfinished wire ends into loops to the back for stringing.

5   Join the three pieces, butted together, with wraps using 1¼" lengths of 22-gauge wire.

6   Use a dowel to shape each piece so they are slightly curved to fit your arm.

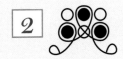

ASSEMBLE THE BRACELET

1   Cut two lengths of 18-gauge wire, each 1½". Make two <u>connectors</u>.

2   Cut two lengths of 20-gauge wire, each 2¼". Make two <u>wrapped bead links</u> using a 6mm silver bead for each.

3   Cut two lengths of flexible beading wire, each 12". Using a crimp bead and crimping pliers, <u>crimp</u> one end of each onto a connector.

4   String the two sides of the bracelet, alternating pebble beads with 2.5mm silver beads, adding on the bead links and jig shapes by stringing through their end loops. Make the piece 7¼" long.

5   Snug up the beads on the wires and crimp the ends onto the remaining connector.

6   Attach a clasp.

Malachite Twist Necklace

FINISHED SIZE: 20"
SKILL LEVEL: Advanced
MATERIALS:

36" strand of malachite chips

2 strands of 11/0 emerald seed beads

24 glass 3–10mm pearl beads

16 glass 10mm pearl beads

5 feet of flexible beading wire

6 crimp beads

21" of 20-gauge wire

5 feet of 18-gauge wire

5/16" dowel

Crimping pliers

Clasp

Needle file or silicon carbide cloth

Wire cutters

Chain nose pliers

Round nose pliers

Pearls, malachite chips and a swirl of wire make a unique blend of sophistication and fun.

STRING THE BEADS

1   Cut two lengths of 20-gauge wire, each 1½". Make two <u>connectors</u>.

2   Cut three lengths of beading wire, each 20". Using the crimp beads and crimping pliers, <u>crimp</u> one end of each to the wrapped loop of a connector.

3   String 12" of beads on each beading wire, alternating seed beads with chips and adding an occasional glass pearl. Crimp each onto the remaining connector.

ASSEMBLE THE NECKLACE

1   Cut eight lengths of 20-gauge wire, each 2¼". Make eight <u>wrapped bead links</u> using the 10mm glass pearl beads. Fasten the wrapped bead links together, making two chains of four links each.

2   Fasten the wrapped bead links to the simple loop of the connector on each side.

3   Cut two lengths of 18-gauge wire, each 30". Hold them together and coil around the dowel.

4   Loosen the coil and work the beaded strands into the interior of the coil; tighten the coils at each end to fit closely around the crimps on the connector.

5   Attach a clasp.

4

Multi-Strand Necklace

FINISHED SIZE: 20¾"

SKILL LEVEL: Advanced

MATERIALS:

Size B black nylon beading thread

Beading needle

1 hank of 11/0 amethyst seed beads

3 feet of 20-gauge copper wire

4 feet of 20-gauge silver wire

10 silver 8mm beads

10 silver 4mm beads with holes that are too small for the seed beads to slip into

Nail polish or glue

Clasp

Needle file or silicon carbide cloth

Wire cutters

Chain nose pliers

Round nose pliers

The wider seed bead sections are a contrast to the tiny-coiled beads in this necklace. Carefully finish the ends of the wire pieces so the threads do not break.

MAKE THE BEADS

1. WOTWS, make five <u>coiled beads</u> out of the copper wire, making them ½" long with a small core (use a 0000 knitting needle or 18-gauge wire).

2. WOTWS, make 10 <u>flat disk beads</u> out of the silver wire, making them about ⅜" in diameter.

STRING THE BEADS

1. Cut 12 lengths of nylon thread, each 36". Tie the lengths of thread together at one end in a loose knot (so the beads will not slide off while you are working).

2. Place the beading needle on one of the threads and string 2" of seed beads followed by the beads shown in the diagram; repeat until there are six sections of seed beads and five sections of the mixed beads. Remove the needle and tie a loose knot.

3. Place the needle on another of the 11 remaining threads. String 2" of seed beads, run the needle through the first section of mixed beads, being careful to not sew through the previous thread, and repeat to the end.

4. Repeat Step 3 for each thread.

FINISH THE NECKLACE

1. Cut two lengths of wire from the 20-gauge wire, each 1½". Make two <u>connectors</u>, making the wrapped loop small and leaving the other end straight.

2. Pass one end of the beaded strands through the wrapped loop of one connector and tie a knot to secure. Saturate the knot with nail polish or glue and allow to dry. Trim the ends to within ⅛" of the knot. Repeat at the other end of the beads.

3. Make two <u>end caps</u> out of 20-gauge wire, placing one on each end of the necklace.

4. Bend the straight end of each connector into a simple loop.

5. Attach a clasp.

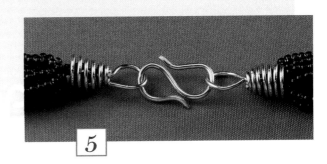

Assemblage Necklace

FINISHED SIZE: 20½"

SKILL LEVEL: Advanced

MATERIALS:

Small tube each of red, yellow, green and blue multi Delica seed beads

Black nylon beading thread

28" of flexible beading wire

4 crimp beads

2⅛" of 18-gauge silver wire

15" of 20-gauge silver wire

7 feet of 20-gauge copper wire

6" of 18-gauge copper wire

12 silver 3mm beads

16 garnet 4mm beads

Beading needle

Clasp

Crimping pliers

Needle file or silicon carbide cloth

Wire cutters

Chain nose pliers

Round nose pliers

Chasing hammer

Anvil

Assorted parts create an artful whole! Follow the instructions, or think up your own ways to combine an assortment of pieces.

MAKE THE BEADED SECTION

1 Follow the <u>Peyote Stitch</u> instructions, stringing on 24 beads in green, and work ¼" plain.

2 Keeping two beads on each side in green, work the center section in blue and red, alternating the colors to form diagonal stripes, and work in this pattern for 1⅜".

3 Change to yellow and red and work the colors alternately for one row.

4 In the following rows, decrease one bead at each edge until one bead remains, then finish off.

5 Turn under the upper edge ¼" and invisibly stitch in place.

MAKE THE BEADS

1 Make six <u>peyote tube beads</u>, stringing the same number of beads as for the pendant, and working the same diagonal pattern as the center of the pendant using red and yellow beads for 12 rows.

2 Cut 16 lengths of 20-gauge copper wire, each 3". Make 16 <u>coil beads</u>, wrapping them around a size 0000 knitting needle or a nail.

3 WOTWS using 20-gauge copper wire, make 12 <u>flat coils</u> ¼" diameter; hammer gently.

4 Make two additional flat coils out of 18-gauge copper wire, ⅜" across; hammer gently.

MAKE THE PENDANT

1 Cut 2⅛" of 18-gauge wire. String the pendant with a larger flat coil on either side of it; bend the ends into loops.

2 Using 20-gauge silver wire, make four <u>simple bead links</u> using two silver beads and a copper coil bead for each.

3 Using a chain nose pliers and 20-gauge copper wire, make four bent hammered dangles 1¼" - 1½" long, fastening one to each bead link. Fasten the two dangles to each end loop of the pendant.

4 Cut four lengths of 20-gauge silver wire, each 2¼". Make four <u>wrapped bead links</u> using a 4mm bead for each. Fasten two to each loop of the pendant.

5 Cut two lengths of flexible beading wire, each 14". String 7½" of beads in the pattern of your choice on each; using crimp beads and a crimping pliers, <u>crimp</u> the ends to the wrapped bead links.

6 Attach a clasp.

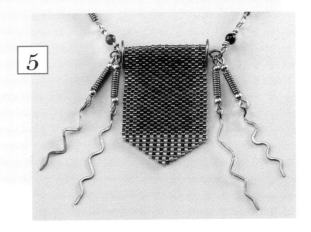

5

Embroidered Cuff

FINISHED SIZE: 7⅜"

SKILL LEVEL: Advanced

MATERIALS:

Lightweight leather, any neutral color, same as pattern plus a 1¼" square piece

Smooth leather for backing, same as pattern plus a 1¼" square piece

7 assorted ½" – ⅝" diameter rounded cabochons

18mm cabochon for the clasp

E6000 glue

Assorted 11/0 and 8/0 seed beads, bugle beads and 4mm beads, in browns, greens, blues, dark reds and purples

18" of 18-gauge wire

Nylon beading thread

Beading needles

Fine sewing needle

Needle file or silicon carbide cloth

Wire cutters

Chain nose pliers

Round nose pliers

Chasing hammer

Anvil

A leather-backed cuff is very comfortable to wear. To custom-fit the bracelet, measure around your wrist and adjust the pattern to make the piece ⅜" longer than your wrist measurement.

INSTRUCTIONS

1 With the 1¼" square of lightweight leather and the 18mm cabochon, sew a <u>beaded bezel</u> using 11/0 seed beads, then sew 8/0 seed beads around the base, then several rounds of 11/0 seed beads, and trim the leather up to the beads.

2 Arrange the seven cabochons onto the larger lightweight leather piece, glue them in place, and allow the glue to dry.

3 Sew a beaded bezel followed by several rounds of 4mm or larger seed beads around the base of each.

4 Sew sections of bugle beads together using <u>ladder stitch</u>, and sew through the beads to stitch them on.

5 WOTWS using 18-gauge wire make several <u>flat coils</u> about ⅜" across, and sew them on randomly by sewing a 4mm bead onto the center of each.

6 Sew on rows of 11/0 seed beads and clusters of <u>fringe stitch</u> using two beads for each to fill in remaining areas.

7 Cut 3" of 18-gauge wire and bend the clasp following the diagram; bend again to form the clasp hook.

8 Cut 2" of 18-gauge wire and bend the clasp loop following the diagram.

9 Stitch the clasp hook to the back of the 18mm cabochon, and the loop end to the square end of the bracelet.

10 Trim to fit, then stitch the backing leather onto the back of the 18mm cabochon, stitching in beading thread using tiny stitches around the edge.

11 Stitch the backing leather onto the back of the larger piece.

12 Stitch the 18mm cabochon securely onto the diagonal end of the bracelet with the clasp facing outwards.

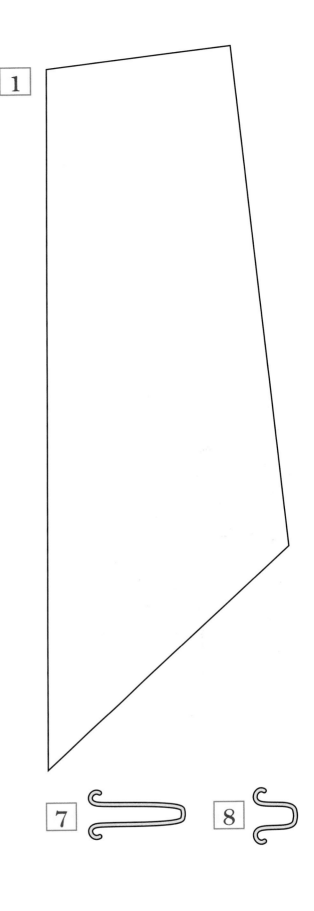

Tapestry Pin and Earrings

FINISHED SIZE: 1⅝" x 4½"

SKILL LEVEL: Advanced

MATERIALS

11/0 Delica seed beads in 8-9 colors of your choice

Size D black nylon beading thread

15" of 18-gauge wire

Pair of ear wires

Beading loom

Needle file or silicon carbide cloth

Wire cutters

Chain nose pliers

Round nose pliers

Chasing hammer

Anvil

Beading needle

Combine colors to make a "landscape painting" in beads. To wear the pin, fasten it so only the very top of the curved wire is caught in the fabric.

Pin

1. Thread the loom with 31 warp threads to make a piece 30 beads wide and work <u>loom beading</u>, starting towards the top of the loom to allow thread length for a 2" fringe.

2. Work four plain rows in any color, then complete the weaving choosing the bead colors as you weave, referring to the photo.

3. When the piece is 1½" long, decrease one bead at each side every row until there are 12 beads across.

4. Remove from the loom and weave in the ends at the top.

5. At the bottom, place the needle onto a thread and string 2" of beads, skip the last bead and run the needle up through all the beads and finish off by weaving in the end. Repeat for the remaining threads.

6. Fold the top four rows to the back and sew in place.

7. Cut 4" of wire. File one end of the wire into a rounded point, so it is not sharp, but will still go through fabric. Place the wire through the casing of the woven piece.

8. Bend ⅜" of the right end of the wire sharply upward; form it into a hook to the back. Bend the left end of the wire into a rounded shape to catch in the hook.

9. Hammer the curved section gently, being careful to avoid the beads.

10. Cut 4" of wire. Bend 3" of one end into a flat coil, place it through the weaving and bend a small coil at the back to hold it in place.

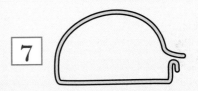

Earrings

1. String the beading loom with two sets of nine threads each to make two pieces each eight beads wide side by side.

2. Weave each piece for 2½", keeping them the same, and choosing the colors as you go. Remove from the loom and work in the threads.

3. Fold the top three rows to the back and sew in place.

4. For each earring, cut 3½" of wire. Hammer 1" of one end, bend the end sharply downwards, and bend a decorative coil.

5. Run the remaining end through the fold of the beaded piece. Bend the end sharply upwards and loosely coil.

6. Attach an ear wire onto the top wire of each.

Earrings Collection 3

Clockwise from top: Triple Oval, Purple Bead, Old Crazy Lace Agate

SKILL LEVEL: Advanced

Make unique earrings by combining individual bent-wire parts and wrapping techniques.

Triple Oval

MATERIALS:

24" of 20-gauge wire

5" of 22-gauge wire

Masking tape

2 matching 6mm or 8mm beads

2 crystal 2mm x 4mm beads

Pair of ear wires

Needle file or silicon carbide cloth

Wire cutters

Chain nose pliers

Round nose pliers

Chasing hammer

Anvil

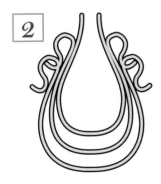

MAKE THE EARRINGS

1 Cut three lengths of 20-gauge wire, each 3". Bend each into an oval shape, bringing the wire ends up.

2 Stack the ovals; tape them together.

3 Cut two lengths of 22-gauge wire, each 1¼". <u>Wrap</u> at each side, and gently hammer the wraps and the ovals.

4 Bend the two outer wires outward to form coiled shapes.

5 Twist the center wire ends together and bend each into a loop with one facing downwards.

6 Cut a 1" length of 20-gauge wire. Make one <u>simple bead drop</u> using one crystal bead and one 6mm or 8mm bead. Fasten the drop to the downward loop.

7 Attach an ear wire.

8 Repeat to make a second earring.

Purple Bead

MATERIALS:

16" of 18-gauge wire

9" of 16-gauge half-round wire

4 silver spacer beads

2 cube-shaped purple beads

Masking tape

Pair of ear wires

Needle file or silicon carbide cloth

Wire cutters

Chain nose pliers

Flat nose pliers

Round nose pliers

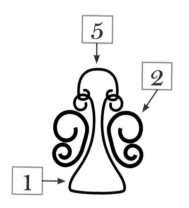

MAKE THE EARRINGS

1 Cut 3" of 18-gauge wire. String a purple bead with a silver spacer on each side; bend the wire according to the diagram.

2 Cut two lengths of 18-gauge wire, each 2". Bend each wire according to the diagram using a round nose pliers.

3 Tape the three pieces together. <u>Wrap</u> the pieces at the center using the half-round wire.

4 Make two additional wraps to stabilize the piece.

5 Cut 1" of 18-gauge wire. Bend the wire in an arc, bending the ends into small loops. Attach this piece to the 3" wire at the top of the earring.

6 Attach an ear wire.

7 Repeat to make a second earring.

Old Crazy Lace Agate

MATERIALS:

19" of 20-gauge wire

10½" of 22-gauge wire

2 Old Crazy Lace agate 6mm beads

Pair of ear wires

Needle file or silicon carbide cloth

Wire cutters

Chain nose pliers

Round nose pliers

Flat nose pliers

Masking tape

MAKE THE EARRINGS

1 Cut 3½" of 20-gauge wire. Bend 2" of one end into a <u>flat coil</u>; string one bead and bend the top into a loop.

2 Cut two lengths of 20-gauge wire, each 3". Shape the wire according to the diagram using a round nose pliers.

3 Tape the three pieces together.

4 Cut 1" of 22-gauge wire. Wrap it beneath the bead.

5 Cut 4¼" of 22-gauge wire. Make a long wrap above the bead.

6 Attach an ear wire.

7 Repeat to make a second earring.

Trio of Hearts Necklace

FINISHED SIZE: 16"
SKILL LEVEL: Advanced
MATERIALS:

- 44" of 18-gauge wire
- 50" of 22-gauge wire
- 2 feet of 16-gauge half-round wire
- 20½" of 20-gauge wire
- 2 jump rings, 6mm
- 2 amethyst 8mm crystal beads
- 9 feet of .5mm tan leather cord
- Masking tape
- Vise or wire twisting tool
- Clasp
- Needle file or silicon carbide cloth
- Wire cutters
- Chain nose pliers
- Flat nose pliers
- Round nose pliers

A trio of hearts makes an eye-catching design. You can vary this necklace to have a single heart by making the braided leather sections longer.

MAKE THE HEARTS

1 Cut two lengths of 22-gauge wire, each 9". Place the lengths in a vise and twist to yield one twisted length.

2 Cut two lengths of 18-gauge wire, each 8". Align the two lengths with the twisted wire in the middle, and tape the ends.

3 <u>Wrap</u> the center of the wire bundle using the half-round wire.

4 Using a chain nose pliers, bend the ends on either side of the wrapping upward, forming a "V" shape, and wrap 1" up from the center on each side.

5 Bend the ends around and to the back, and then upward at the sides, and tape the ends.

6 Cut 2" of half-round wire and <u>wrap</u> where the two circles come together at the center of the heart.

7 Wrap again about 1" away, leaving the shortest end about ⅝" long.

8 Trim all the ends to no more than ¾" and curl the lower two ends downward.

9 Curl the upper end upward.

10 Follow Steps 1-9 to make two more hearts a little smaller, using two 8" lengths of 22-gauge, and a 7" length of 18-gauge wire for each.

11 Fasten the three hearts together with two jump rings fastened to the upper loops of each heart.

MAKE THE WRAPPED BEAD LINKS

1 Cut two lengths of 20-gauge wire, each 2¼". Make two <u>wrapped bead links</u> using an amethyst crystal bead for each.

2 Fasten a wrapped bead link to each end of the hearts piece.

BRAID THE CORD

1 Cut nine lengths of leather cord, each 6"; tape them together about 1" from one end. Using 4" of 20-gauge wire, make a <u>cord end</u> on the taped end.

2 Fasten the loop into a bench vise. Divide the cords into groups of three and braid.

3 Make a cord end at the other end, fastening it to the wrapped bead link as you make the link.

4 Make a braid the same for the other side of the necklace.

5 Attach a clasp.